AF541498

SOCIOLOGY

CULTURE AND NATURE OF SOCIAL CHANGE

Edited by
R. Yadav

Omega Publications
NEW DELHI - 110 002 (INDIA)

OMEGA PUBLICATIONS
4378/4B, G-4, JMD House,
Murari Lal Street, Ansari Road,
Daryaganj, New Delhi-110 002
Phone: 65901906, 9811787417 (M)
e-mail: omega_publications@yahoo.com

Head Office:
79/3, Laxmi Garden,
Near Satya Jyoti School,
Gurgaon (Haryana).

Sociology: Culture and Nature of Social Change

First Published, 2010

ISBN: 978-81-8455-199-0

PRINTED IN INDIA

Printed at Tarun Offset Press, Delhi-110053

PREFACE

This textbook, intended for use in the first college course in sociology, is not designed for solo reading by the student. It is not a series of essays presenting the latest and most "interesting" findings in each of the fields of sociological study. Nor is it an encyclopedic compilation of up-to-the-minute facts and figures relating to the contemporary social scene. It embodies, rather, an approach to sociology which emphasizes the systematic use of an organized and consistent method of investigation.

Out of the possible central themes which might acceptably integrate the system of basic sociological concepts developed in the text, the authors have chosen the triad: interaction, function, and coordination. Their own experience indicates that the student who grasps the significance of these concepts and of their interrelation is stimulated to further fruitful investigation of what is accomplished in the societal mode of life.

Background and Presentation. Observation and logical inference from observation form the background of the statements made in the text. This is an empirical study of society. Of necessity, every statement about reality implies a definitephilosophical position regarding the nature and knowability of reality. In this connection, the authors acknowledge themselves to be moderate realists, maintaining that there is reality beyond the immediate data of sense perceptions, and that such reality is knowable. However, they have tried to hew close to the somewhat elusive line which marks the boundary between empirical science and metaphysics. For instance, when the concept of the social "nature" of man is introduced, the borderline has been touched; but the metaphysical implications of the concept of "nature" are not pursued, and the student is led immediately back to the level of observation.

This arrangement is not only logically imperative; it also parallels, the authors believe, the course of reasoning of the men who have formulated the body of knowledge called sociology. The propositions of sociology were not derived immediately from research conducted with the aid of refined scientific apparatus. They are the end product of a process which started with knowledge originally gained through participant observation in concrete social systems, then refined through the common scientific procedures of comparison, classification, and generalization. In turn, the propositions thus formulated have served as the basis of conceptual schemes guiding technical research, the results of which partly verify, partly invalidate the initial propositions. In consequence, the propositions are modified and made more specific, to be used as starting points for still further research. This process is still going on. The beginning student is unable to grasp the significance of the complicated and highly specialized research which forms the latter stages of the process. But if he follows this course, from very simple observations of the family to generalizations concerning the whole range of social facts, he goes the same way, if not as far as the accomplished man of science. This, in itself, is an important phase of the process of acquiring the habit of mind proper to any scientific discipline.

— Editor

Contents

1

CULTURE AS CIVILIZATION

There are nearly as many definitions of sociology as there are writers of sociological books. In general it is not wise to attempt a definition of a subject in the first pages of a book designed to teach others what the subject is; definitions more properly come at the end. Yet there must be a starting point, and it may well be the assumption that underlies all definitions of sociology, no matter how divergently these are worded: man, as a social being, behaves. A second assumption, also implicit in the various definitions of sociology, is that the behavior of man as a member of a group is different from the behavior of man without social contacts. Man, the human being, is different from man, the animal. There is the further assumption implicit in the publication of books on sociology that social behavior can be studied. For preliminary purposes sociology may be defined as the study of behavior of men in their group life. Included in this would be the study of the relations between individuals, groups, and the group and the individual.

A casual survey of man the world over indicates that the social behavior varies from place to place. Japanese boys and girls are unlike American boys and girls, and the difference is not only that of skin color. Far more fundamental are differences in *civilization*. Civilization may be defined as " the mode of life " of a people. We lead a life far different from that led by our ancestors who lived at the time of George Washington; our mode of life is different; our civilization is different in many significant aspects. In sociological literature the word *culture* is employed to designate what in more popular language we term civilization; sometimes the words *cultural heritage* are employed. All three are synonymous; we shall most often employ the word culture in the pages that follow.

To understand the social behavior of man, it is necessary to understand culture, for the social life of man is rooted in his culture, and depends upon it.

It is essential first to become aware that culture is not inborn; modes of life are not acquired through germinal inheritance. Culture is passed on from generation to generation by a process of social transmission, and is totally unrelated to biological transmission. This point is clarified by George A. Dorsey further on in this volume. It is sometimes difficult to recognize this, especially in our own habituated behavior. As Dr. Franz Boas has said:

We are accustomed to consider all those actions that are part and parcel of our own culture, standards which we follow automatically, as common to all mankind. They are deeply ingrained in our behavior. We are moulded in their forms so that we cannot think but that they must be valid everywhere. . . . Much of what we ascribe to human nature is no more than a reaction to the restraints put upon us by our civilization.

Put in other words, this all means that man as an animal is born into a civilization, acquires a mode of life, builds habits that reflect this culture, and becomes thoroughly a product of it.

Culture can be analyzed, and the ethnologist, working

among primitive groups, and the sociologist, working in contemporary societies, both aim to understand the mechanisms of culture by careful analysis. While any culture may be regarded as a unity, examination will show it to be composed of minuter parts all woven together and interrelated. The parts are ways of doing things, ways of thinking, and material objects that men utilize in their lives. These elements, material and non-material, are called *culture traits.* In their entirety, these culture traits, as man adapts himself and absorbs them, constitute the mode of life of the group. As these traits differ, in number or in elaboration, the mode of life of any group will differ.

One writer has put this ably in these words:

The sequence of changes in the " make-up " in this or that group of men we call their "past"; and the expressions of such "make-up" in this or that group of men, living in these or those surroundings, we call their " culture "; that is to say, the way they look after themselves and one another, and the way they look *at* that which is not themselves. For " culture " is not a state or a condition only, but a process; as in *agriculture* or *horticulture* we mean not the condition of the land but the whole round of the farmer's year, and all that he does in it; "culture," then, is what remains of men's past, working on their present, to shape their future.

The most important phases of culture can be described as of five kinds: geographical, temporal, functional, psychological, and valua-tional. However, new interests necessitate new classifications and orientations, and it is not possible to make an exhaustive or a perpetually satisfying list of the referential meanings of culture phases or culture traits.

Yet (1) each culture has a geographical location. Even philosophic theories and scientific achievements can be described in terms of geographical distribution. (2) Geographical classification easily passes over into temporal, that is, history supplements geography. In many cases the longer a trait exists the further it travels; and independently of the geographical reference, culture facts can be arranged in a time order which gives them historical significance. Culture, in short, can be viewed as history. (3) A trait can be viewed in its functional relation to human culture or to the culture to which it immediately belongs. It can be oriented with regard to its prominence in the culture, the extent to which it has developed, or in other manner. (4) The prominence of the culture trait in the psychological life of the people, its effect upon their mentality, and their reactions to it, give the psychological placement. (5) The trait can be viewed in relation to its value to the immediate culture and to human life. The canoe, for example, is a thing of value as well as a trait which has geographical distribution, historical development, utility in the immediate culture, and psychological appeal. The unique characteristic of human evolution lies in the creation by man of culture.

Man has perfected in the course of his evolution certain methods of social cooperation [modes of life] which have completely transformed individual behavior and individual experience. The inner life of a human being is not merely the inner life of an animal somewhat enlarged in scale; the constant use of words, the resort to tools, and respect for justice have produced so fundamental a change in the character of consciousness that man and animals must be described as essentially different.

Such are the transforming powers of culture, such the influences upon man's behavior.

There have been many approaches to the study of man's social behavior. To some the geographical setting has seemed all-important. Were we historians we might be concerned primarily with the historical processes that are involved. As psychologists we should be prone to stress the psychological factors. But underlying all of these is a cultural setting. Physical environment is transformed by man's handiwork; the historical processes operate in a cultural environment; the very content of the mind reflects the social heritage. There is no denial that each of these is important; neither is it to be denied that a cultural approach is fruitful. In the end sociology must be justified by its fruits, for these constitute the value of its pursuits. In this book a cultural approach will dominate, and the attempt will be made to show the significance of culture in human behavior. Culture itself will be studied, for culture has developed and is constantly changing; it has its history, and its condition at any moment is in large part the outcome of historical processes. Cultures, like individuals, have pasts as well as a present, and the present is always shaped by the past.

The writers who are quoted in this first chapter emphasize the importance of the cultural approach in analyzing social life, and probably all of them would agree that it is the most promising of approaches in attempting to understand social life. The sections by Dorsey and Goldenweiser define culture. Kroeber stresses the importance of culture in shaping life, and aims to orient the student in his subsequent study. He makes clear the difficulty of seeing one's own culture and of studying it with objectivity. The discussion of food prejudices by Townsend demonstrates how thoroughly culture permeates the individual's behavior; culture is not only a matter of material objects, it involves the basic responses of life in ways that are exceedingly subtle.

The cultural approach to social life also throws into different relief the contrast in behavior between our own and simpler peoples. Ethnologists now argue that human behavior in primitive times was much the same as today. Goldenweiser has said, "Man is one; civilizations are many." The unity of the human mind is becoming an accepted fact. It is cultures that vary. Five selections develop this thought in more detail: Wallis, Boas, and Wissler state a theoretical position, and Linton and Young trace the evolution of two manifestations of contemporary totemism.

WHAT IS CULTURE?

The Smith-family-Eobinson are ashore for a picnic on an island never before trod by Man. All go in for a swim. A tidal wave picks them up and drops them far inland, leaving no trace of boat, ship, or anything but the scant whatever they had on. The shock robs them of all memory of past life. They do not even remember their own names.

Once Man was like that. Nature had made him, but Man himself had not made anything. All that he has made since is culture.

Man made culture because culture seemed the easiest way to satisfy a force within. This force was the joy of life, the love to live. It drove him to get on, to try to make life more secure, to rise above and become less dependent upon physical surroundings; to postpone, to cheat, death.

He improved his lot. One thing led to another. Meanwhile he talked the situation over with his mate, parents, children, friends. One word led to another — a new word for each new tool, for every new situation. He invented a language — many languages.

Customs became established into rules for living together, rules for family life, rules to govern the group. He invented Heads of houses, Chiefs of tribes, Priests of religion — for he early took to religion.

He so loved life and had so little confidence in his own power that he sought power everywhere — in stones, in rivers, in trees, from the Serpent, from the Eagle, from Sun, Moon, and Stars. He peopled his world with ghosts — propitiated those he feared, cajoled those he hated. Anything to get more power —power over foes, over dangers, over forces, over life, over death.

He would cheat death. He would make life more secure, more stable. The quest for life led him a merry chase. It leads us a merry chase. It might be so much merrier.

Man must eat, drink, and be married — or he dies and leaves no mourners. It almost looks like a vicious circle. In a way it is — in this way: we always get back to the nature of the beast, to human nature, to the nature of life. Nature does not" believe " in civilization, vote the Republican ticket, or set kings on or off thrones. Nature is interested in food and sleep, legs and livers, and babies. Nor does she care what or when we eat — only that we get enough of certain foods; nor with whom we mate — only that we propagate our kind.

Life is simple. It is Man that is complex — complex in the vast and intricate machinery he has devised to satisfy Life's simple demands. Wonderful machinery — but are we always certain we know what it is all about, what it does to us, whether we fit into it, whether it fits us?

This machinery is Man-made, " artificial " — it has a history. Man is a product of Nature, " natural " — Man has a history. The two histories are not the same. One is millions of years long, the other but a few weeks as time flies. One begins where the other leaves off. One is Nature, the other is culture. Culture takes a thousand forms and goes by many names. Its forms change and often have but little relation to the work they were asked to do. The work to be done is always the same: satisfy Man's love of life and need for love. Culture is handed down to us from loving.hands — it is our partimony. Often we do not see it, we just accept it with child-like faith, assuming that it is what we want, what we need, all that we can get. We lean on it to get us food and sleep and rest and immortality. We count on it for support, as our ancestors counted on the spirits they propitiated with food and wine. We even throw a halo over it, venerate it, sanctify it. Or, we try to improve it, not knowing what we try to improve, not realizing that Man is of more value than custom or law.

Culture is the means to the ends of life. The ends are rooted in our natural inheritance. The understanding of that inheritance is the key to human culture; without that key we cannot unlock the chests of our social patrimony, nor separate the gold from the base metal of our lives.

CULTURE AS CIVILIZATION

What, then, is civilization?

Our attitudes, beliefs and ideas, our judgments and values; our institutions, political and legal, religious and economic; our ethical code and our code of etiquette; our books and machines, our sciences, philosophies and philosophers — all of these and many other things and beings, both in themselves and in their multiform interrelations, constitute our civilization. In many of these things it differs from the civilizations of antiquity and from those other remoter ones of pre-history.

It is characteristic of civilization that it persists; a large part of it, most of it, in fact, is passed on from generation to generation. But also it changes; at no two points in time is it quite the same, and the differences in the civilization of two succeeding generations are often perceptible and at times striking.

It takes but little thought to realize that the changes in civilization are each and all due to the emergence of new things: inventions, ideas, which, in the last analysis, are always emanations of the minds of individuals. Whether the change is in a mechanical device or a detail of social organization; in a new scientific idea or ethical value; in a method of simplifying or improving economic production or distribution; in a new play or a novel form of stage art; in an article of use, comfort, or luxury, a new word, a witticism, a proverb — all of these things originate in individual minds and there is no other place where they can originate. Nor is this generalization in the least affected by whatever view one may hold as to the relative importance of the individual and society in the production of civilization. Even though the individual were wholly determined by the social setting, all of the civil-izational changes just referred to, including those in material things, would remain psychological in their derivation and, as such, they could only originate in individual minds, for there are no other minds but those of individuals. Thus the whole of civilization, if followed backward step by step, would ultimately be found resolvable, without residue, into bits of ideas in the minds of individuals.

But civilization also persists and accumulates. Some elements carry over from generation to generation through the sheer objective continuity of material existence. Most of the paraphernalia of our complicated mechanical equipment, the roads, vehicles, and houses, the books in our libraries, the specimens in the museums, persist in as crass and material a way as does man's physical environment. The institutions, those crystallized depositories of attitudes, ideas, and actions, persist in a less objectified form; for they are only in part represented by material or mechanical arrangements, such as fixed organizations, recorded codes, and archives in whose prolonged existence the change of generations appears as but an incident. But there is still another and more important mechanism through which civilization is passed on from fathers to sons This mechanism, more dynamic and plastic than the others is education Through education, in the home, at school, in society, the past molds the present and sets a pattern for the future.

Here it is important to remember that civilization, psychological and individual though it may be when resolved into a chronological series, is not at all the outgrowth of the minds of individuals of any particular generation. On the contrary. It comes to them from without; it molds them; it forces itself upon them through the material persistence of its objective elements, through its codes and institutions, and through the deep cutting tools of education. A large part of the educational process strikes the mind of the individual during the years of highest receptivity and plasticity. Without accepting the extreme verdict of psychoanalysis on this matter, it suffices to realize that what is deposited in the mind during the early years of childhood persists throughout later life with often but slight modification.

Not only is man at the mercy of civilization, but he generally remains either partly or wholly unaware of what he is thus forced to accept.

While we regard the language in which we think and express our ideas as very particularly our own, the grammatical structure of that language rests in the unconscious. The complicated systems of classification, categories, and nuances which make up grammar are used by the individual without the least realization of their presence. In primitive communities where writing is unknown individuals are totally unaware of the very existence of a grammar underlying the language they daily use. The situation is not so very different today, for the fact that grammar is taught does not prevent us from absorbing the structure of our mother tongue without the least reference to whatever conscious knowledge we may acquire of its grammatical principles. Only at the cost of a deliberate and persistent effort can the mind be brought to deal analytically with the elements of the grammar it constantly employs in thinking.

The same is almost equally true of art, particularly of music. The theoretical structure of our musical system is known to but few. Many of those who appreciate music or even produce it by singing or playing the instrument may remain almost wholly unconscious of the basic principles under which they operate. And, again, in primitive society or among the singing and banjo-playing masses of our cities, the theoretical foundations of the music they enjoy, use, and abuse, remain altogether unknown. What applies so drastically to language and art is only to a slighter degree true of other elements of civilization. Rules of etiquette, religious dogma, political convictions, and to a great extentthe specialized outlook of a social or professional class, become fixed in the mind of the individual before he is quite aware of what is taking place.

Then, when self-consciousness comes — and to many of us it never comes — we discover ourselves fitted out with all the paraphernalia of a world view, with a code of morality, behavior, and belief. Then we may indulge in a deliberate effort to change these ideas and attitudes or, more commonly, to provide for them an exculpating background of explanations and justifications. Many of our theories of education, of criminology, or of etiquette, for example, consist of nothing but such accumulated afterthoughts, invented with greater or less ingenuity to render our unconsciously acquired habits, attitudes, and convictions more congenial to ourselves and better prepared to hold their own in the face of criticism or attack.

It appears from the above that the individual and the group have their share both in the persistence and the origination of civilization. The individual is responsible for the creation of the new; society provides it with a background and the occasion. For the new is never more than a slight ripple on the deep foundation of the old and established. The conservative dead-weight of society opposes the new, but, should it appear, molds it to its pattern by prescribing the direction it is to take as well as by limiting the range of its departure from the old. This is most clearly seen in inventions and artistic creations. The talent of an Edison is a congenital gift. Even though born in early pre-history, he would have been Edison, but could not have invented the incandescent lamp. Instead, he might have originated one of the early methods of making fire. Raphael, if brought to life in a Bushman family, would have drawn curiously realistic cattle on the walls of caves as well as steatopygous Bushmen women. Had Beethoven been a Chinaman, he would have composed some of those delightfully cacophonous melodies which the seeker for the quaint and unusual pretends to enjoy in Chinatown.

Stability and persistence, on the other hand, are mainly brought about by social factors. Apart from the historic institutional norms and the directing pressure of public opinion, custom and law are functions of the social setting. But these factors alone would be powerless to achieve stability in the absence of the inertia of the individual mind, with its readiness to adhere to once established conceptions and its predilection for the beaten path.

A civilization in its unique individuality is fascinating to behold and to study. This charm of specific cultural values eluded the eye of the evolutionist of a generation ago, whose interest centered in the task of reconstructing the antecedents of modern society. To him the civilizations of antiquity, and to an even greater degree those of pre-history, were but stepping-stones on the road to modern civilization, but stages in an ascending series of development. The modern student, whether historian, sociologist, or anthropologist, having freed himself from the dogmatic preconceptions of the evolutionary approach, is seized with renewed zeal toward a better understanding and deeper penetration of the total range of human civilization. But the data for his study are limited. Beneath manifold differences, a level of great uniformity underlies all modern civilizations. A comparison of the latter with those of antiquity contributed a wider range of contrasting colors; but the number of such ancient civilizations is small, and, on analysis, they also display many common elements with our own. Pre-history, as it stands revealed by the researches of the ethnographer, belongs to a totally different plane. Each one of its civilizations is individual and unique, is carried by relatively few individuals, and covers but slight territory. Of such highly individualized civilizations, pre-history reveals a great variety, even though the list be made to include only those tribes whose cultural possessions have been studied with care and in detail. Primitive North America alone comprises a greater number of well authenticated civilizations than can be found in the whole range of modern and ancient history.

The early world, then, presents an ideal field for the study of the achievements of man, for the extension of our understanding of cultural problems, and our appreciation of the great range of civilization.

THE CULTURAL POINT OF VIEW

The business of putting across what detachment from culture really implies is not an easy one. The individual who happens to be detached already needs no explanation. Those who are not do not feel this detachment, and words about it tend to glance off unperceived. In most deeper relations, we are all unconscious of the hold which our culture has on us. It is from our culture that we derive our standards; it is our culture that incessantly shapes our behavior, to the extent of determining the form of expression of all impulses — conditioning all responses, as we say nowadays.

A partial illustration may help. Illiterate people know nothing of grammar; but they invariably speak consistently to some grammatical scheme. Popular usage is misleading here. When we ordinarily refer to " ungrammatical speech," we mean speech which does not follow the code of rules standardized and accepted as correct. We do not mean that people who say " them guys " and " I ain't saw him " follow no rules at all. At least we have no reason to mean it: they plainly follow rules of their own. Just so, all known languages possess a grammar; those of tribes without writing are often exceedingly intricate in structure, though none of the speakers are any more aware of the fact than of their having a cortex with nine billion cells inside their heads. A good nervous system functions without knowing its existence, and a good language functions equally well whether its rules — its structure and processes — have or have not been formulated.

In short, grammar — as a fact — is always there; grammarians may or may not come along to record it. Mostly, in the history of the world, they have not. When they have, they have always found something astonishingly determinative of how people will say what they have to say. The impulse to express this or that has nothing to do with linguistics. But how we say it, and therefore literally what we say — the actual objective phenomena of utterance — depend directly and immediately on linguistic factors — rules of grammar and the like.

Now, the same is true of culture to nearly the same degree. The naive person in any culture accepts his culture without analysis. He feels it as part of himself, something that is in him. Those phases of a culture which concern him he appropriates for his functioning, makes his own; the others he ignores. Result: he scarcely knows that the culture exists except through his personal utilization of it. Whoever departs from the standards and norms which he has appropriated arouses disapproval of much the same kind as he who murders his mother tongue. The naive person is interested, perhaps excited, about such deviations; but it is the deviations, not the standards, that arouse his attention. The standards are taken for granted; they are felt with immediacy.

So far we are still within the limits of one culture. When human beings of a different culture are encountered, they and their ways and the standards obviously inherent in their wavs tend to be observed first with wonder, then with amusement, in the end usually with irritation or contempt. But the naive man, who is the " normal " man, is thereby no nearer an intellectual detachment from his own culture. He may be more tolerant for knowing strange customs and standards; he is not likely to be appreciably more introspective or analytical.

To revert to our parallel, grammar no doubt existed in human speech for several tens of thousands of years without being dreamed of; grammar as a conscious dissection of one's own speech — Greek or Sanskrit — is barely two thousand years old; comparative philology is but a hundred and fifty. And comparative philology is still mainly Indo-Germanic — the study of the sisters and cousins of our own idiom. True comparative linguistics, — depersonalized, denationalized, de-occiden-talized, — the unpartisan examination of any and all languages with an interest in the total range and variability of their forms and processes, is yet in its infancy.

And so is depersonalized, denationalized, de-occidentalized culture investigation. History as *de facto* studied, written, and read is, Robinson's and Spengler's philippics notwithstanding, ninety-nine per cent the history of the culture movement of which our Western culture of the century is a mere variant. Economics virtually begins its operations with the French Revolution, mostly, in fact, not until about 1830. This is not a stricture. It is natural to be interested in oneself and one's own; possibly it is healthiest; certainly it is practical. Only it does not make for really understanding oneself.

Now, what is this culture about which it is so hard or unnatural to be self-conscious? It is the product of men as they live in groups or societies. It exists only by virtue of men existing; but it exists as something over and above them. Flaherty, Greenbaum, and Patucci are individuals and remain such; but Flaherty, Greenbaum, and Patucci as directors of the Enterprise Development Company, Inc., have given rise to something super-individual, and their acts as the association have a cogency and produce results which are legally, economically, emotionally tangible. This is not a far-fetched parallel except at one point. The incor-porators deliberately take a step, certain of the conditions of which are precisely regulated; and they take it for specific purposes. Whereas you, reader, and I, writer, along with Flaherty, Greenbaum, Patucci, and all others, are constantly and involuntarily, with and without legal sanction, sometimes with but mostly without awareness, producing culture: fortifying, hardening, altering, innovating this or that " way " of pur time and civilization.

Culture has been defined as a detritus of living: a precipitate to which all generations contribute. It is that and more. Each generation is reared and lives in the precipitate of its forerunners. Unknowingly and inevitably it adapts itself to the environment of this social precipitate as it adapts itself to the environment of its climate. And by adding its quota of further precipitate it starts its successor off in a somewhat different cultural environment. Law, religion, manners, tastes are never quite the same. Even in an ultra-conservative period in which they did not change formally — to take an unattainable example — they would acquire added age and therewith weight to steady or oppress the next generation.

Culture then, while it exists only through men or in men, has an existence of its own. It has not got a sensory reality in the sense that blood in the veins or salt water in the ocean has; but it exists, just as truly as, say, tuberculosis, or credit, or momentum. What is more, culture produces, through the men whom it affects, more or new culture; and is therefore a cause as well as an effect, a stimulus as well as a residuum. It is for this reason that the words detritus and precipitate are not wholly satisfactory as descriptions of it.

They convey too much the idea of a mere by-product, whereas culture is creative as well as created. Spencer coined a happy word for it in superorganic; only, having neatly illustrated what he meant thereby, he put the concept back onthe shelf and proceeded to explain sociological phenomena mainly by organic or pseudo-organic mechanisms.

One more analogy. We can conceive culture as like a coral reef — dead matter, the mere secretions of past generations, but none the less actual. What is more, the reef determines the life of the polyps on it. They can survive only within a narrow fringe of its oceanward crest. As they live and grow, the reef alters and presents new living surfaces, new possibilities, to their descendants. The reef is wholly the product of polyps; but it also determines the conditions and manner of existence of all individual polyps. Culture is just as actual and just as determining as the reef. And it is just as distinct from human beings as the reef is distinct from the living polyps on its upper edge.

A polyp who conceived the idea that he was a free, self-determining being, able to do what he pleased and to contribute as he liked to the growth of his "civilization" — the reef—would impress us as a somewhat shortsighted and egocentric polyp. If he despised the reef as " dead," well, that would be his privilege while alive, but it would not argue for his perspective of vision nor indicate that he understood the relations of things in the world or his relation to them.

From the point of view of what is organic, there are only men and polyps; culture and the reef are mere environment. But from an angle other than the organic — call it superorganic or anything else — the precipitate is not only a far bigger thing than the aggregation of all the individuals of one time, but has a history of its own, an immensely long history; and it necessarily influences the basic fortunes, the actual life histories, of all the individuals of any generation.

Once such an idea of culture has been conceived, one becomes an humbler personality. Thinking oneself god, or even potential god, in relation to humanity, comes to seem an infantility. It is not that the results of biology and psychology are minimized by the concept of culture. They retain full significance, but an understanding is superadded which these approaches alone cannot yield. The grandeur, the pervasive influence of this superorganic precipitate, the fact that it can be apperceived from one aspect as essentially self-sufficient, as almost self-determining, cannot but react on thought and ultimately on living. One begins to see what history is — the record of a set of processes or forces that shape humankind.

One realizes, too, how right those are who wish to reform history; how temperate in fact. The history that has come down to us and passes current is that of the western half of a continental annex plus little corners of two adjacent continents. It goes back barely twenty-five hundred years. Half of it is political — all the other aspects of culture crowded into the other and perhaps lesser half — because the approach is primarily through political documents. And what it contains of culture is almost inextricably mixed with biographies of personalities, sometimes with ethical or social or national propaganda.

The problem follows how the inquiring attitude as to culture came about. This is a matter that is far from clear. The main point which emerges with sureness is that it is an unusual happening for a culture to be interested in culture as such. The ancients lacked the interest altogether. Herodotus can be called the first ethnologist as well as the father of history — but with the same half appropriateness only. He was interested in customs, the stranger the better. But it was the marveling of a child at an elephant, or at the story of a dragon; it was not an attempt to understand. Herodotus was fascinated by the endless panorama of ethnic custom and variety, as he was by the kaleidoscope of historic events; but he scarcely attempted to interpret. He liked, naively and with freshness, to deal with the raw materials of culture. He lived too early to found a science of culture. And the other ancients lacked even his spontaneous interest: Greek culture was a pretty well self-absorbed affair.

Lucretius, carrying on one of the traditions of Greek philosophy, speculated a little as to the origins of fire, tools, worship, belief in gods, the state. He did not recognize culture as such. Arts and institutions were something that flowed of themselves, or by accident, from the original nature of man — from his fingers and claws, his naked skin, his greed and his fear, his dreams. The sense of problem rests lightly on Lucretius as on every good system builder.

The Middle Ages were too ignorant and provincial to be concerned; the Renaissance too creative and too taken up with its expansion of its cosmos. The Seventeenth Century became conscious of science; the Eighteenth began to see an opportunity in savage and strange nations. They were a tool with which to pry into our own culture, a club with which to beat it. There was a sudden interest in China for the comparisons it afforded. Voltaire brought Turks and Hurons on the scene as well as Syrians; and Rousseau his unspoiled savage. Then followed the romantic savage. But these ethnic aliens were dragged into view for reference back to our culture, not from an interest in problems concerned with their own. Voltaire fundamentally cared no more about Hurons than Tacitus about Germans. But Hurons and Germans were effective weapons with which to attack the society and manners of France and Rome.

The Nineteenth Century, accordingly, in which scientific interest in culture as such had its birth, found itself fairly will stocked with knowledge of all sorts of cultures, and much untutored, emotionally tinged interest in them lying about. It is not clear precisely what caused the century to try to deal scientifically with these cultures and thereupon with culture as such. In part it may have been an automatic extension of the procedure of science, then entering into its period oftriumph. Another factor may have been a backwash from the rising tide of nationalism. The fading of religious values almost certainly contributed, at least by removing obstacles; for religions that are believed or even habitually professed necessarily set up values of superiority which block impartial comparative inquiry. But as specific causes these explanations seem inadequate. The phenomenon is perhaps too near us, too much still part of us, for satisfactory analysis to be possible.

The anthropologists that have been the most formally accredited representatives of the movement to inquire into culture have been a curious lot, with strangely heterogeneous motivations. There were essential collectors, to whom the assemblage of varied data was fascinating. There were lovers of the exotic; there were mystics. Bastian was something of each; it would not be unfair to say that Sir James Frazer has inclinations in the same three directions. Anthropologists are still broken up into schools that have little in common except subject matter. There are the functionalists like Radcliffe Brown and Malinowski, essentially reverting to the old basis of reducing culture phenomena to the original nature of man. The historical reconstructionists have broken with psychology and trace the plan of what happened; some, like Nordenskiold and Wissler, with cautious induction; others, such as Elliot Smith and Father Schmidt, with a running start of hypothesis. The historical realists, such as Laufer, are equally broad in their interests, but scarcely venture beyond the documentation that is available. Still others, Boas for instance, distrust both the psychological and the reconstructing historical methods and aim at isolating processes of cultural events with little interest in the place of these events in actual time arid space. This school stands nearest to the exact sciences.

However, only a fraction of the study given to culture is in the hands of anthropologists. H. G. Wells and Oswald Spengier, who know better than to claim the title, are fired by an intense interest to understand - culture, and have contributed insight and perspective. Some of the most valuable work has come from special interests: Taylor on the alphabet, Fergusson on architecture, for example. And many an archaeologist who has never formulated a general concept about what culture is or how it may behave has contributed valuably, and often more sanely than many an anthropologist. The avowed anthropologist, by and large, tends to be queer; as the psychologist inclines to be inhibited, the biologist fanatical, the physicist naive.

One of the great nationalities of the West has stood nearly aloof from the current of interest in culture as such: France. In concrete archaeology, as in history, which can be successfully pursued without many implications, the French easily hold their own; in ethnology, descriptive or interpretative, they hang back. Apparently they are too interested in their own culture to care much about understanding others.

Darwinism is often spoken of as allied to anthropological thought. There is no specific connection. The one deals with biological phenomena and processes; the other begins where these leave off. The common element is the wholly generic concept of evolution, equally applicable in astronomy and geology. Organic evolution is essentially modificatory, cultural evolution cumulative. The one is bound up with heredity, the other in principle is free from it. The similarity is merely a loose analogy, and the Darwinian point of view has retarded and confused the understanding of culture.

Sociology has followed neighboring paths; but they have been paths of its own, which are only beginning to connect. To begin with, sociology, as its name implies, has been concerned primarily with society, not with culture. Secondly, sociology began with the idea that there was a progress in values, and that itself stood as the pinnacle of the sciences. The tinging with values has persisted. Much of sociology is still concerned with reform and amelioration. Its aim is to serve. It remains an applied science without essential foundation in a specific pure science. These statements do not apply to all sociologists. There is a visible breaking away from the habits of applying value standards and bettering conditions. Given time, sociology even promises to outlive the effects of its siring by a propagandist philosopher. When it becomes a pure science it ought to be the cardinal one of all those concerned with culture.

I have spoken of the anthropological attitude in default of a better term. In the development of this attitude, recognized anthropology plays a part. All in all it is a small part; that of a vehicle in a procession, more or less. One cannot possess the feel of culture without realizing that anything organized, professionalized, is only an instrument or expression of the real currents that move underneath. What is significant is an attitude of mind. This attitude anthropologists perhaps do ~ most to sharpen.

But the energy and potentiality of the attitude are widespread — diffused through and rooted in the whole culture of the present day.

2

CULTURE AND PSYCHOLOGY

THE STUDY OF CULTURE : CULTURE AND PSYCHOLOGY

With the beginning of the European war the word " culture " acquired a sense in popular English usage which had long prevailed in ethnological literature. Culture is, indeed, the sole and exclusive subject-matter of ethnology, as consciousness is the subject-matter of psychology, life of biology, electricity of a branch of physics. Culture shares with these other fundamental concepts the peculiarity that it can be properly understood only by an enlarged familiarity with the facts it summarizes. There is no royal shortcut to a comprehension of culture as a whole by definition any more than to a comprehension of consciousness; but as every analysis and explanation of particular conscious states adds to our knowledge of what consciousness is, so every explanation of particular cultural phenomena adds to our insight into the nature of culture. We must, however, start with some proximate notion of what we are to discuss, and for this purpose Tylor's definition in the opening sentence of his *Primitive Culture* will do as well as any: " Culture . . . is that complex whole which includes knowledge, belief, art, morals, law, custom, and any other capabilities and habits acquired by man as a member of society."

For purely practical reasons, connected with the minute division of labor that has become imperative with modern specialization, ethnology has in practice concerned itself with the cruder cultures of peoples without a knowledge of writing. But this division is an illogical and artificial one. As the biologist can study life as manifested in the human organism as well as in the amoeba, so the ethnologist might examine and describe the usages of modern America as well as those of the Hopi Indians. In these lectures I shall therefore not hesitate to draw upon illustrations from the higher civilizations where these seem most appropriate.

Indeed, it may be best for pedagogical reasons to commence with an enumeration of instances of cultural activity in our own midst. And since there is a persistent tendency to associate with culture the more impressive phenomena of art, science, and technology, it is well to insist at the outset that these loftier phases are by no means necessary to the concept of culture. The fact that your boy plays " button, button, who has the button? " is just as much an element of our culture as the fact that a room is lighted by electricity. So is the baseball enthusiasm of our grown-up population, so are moving picture shows, *thes dansants*, Thanksgiving Day masquerades, bar-rooms, Ziegfeld Midnight Follies, evening schools, the Hearst papers, woman suffrage clubs, the single-tax movement, Riker drug stores, touring-sedans, and Tammany Hall.

These, then, represent the type of phenomena comprised under the caption of culture. They exist, and science, as a complete view of reality, cannot ignore them. But a question ominous for the worker who derives his bread and butter from ethnological investigation arises. All the phenomena mentioned and the rest of the same order relate to man, and they relate to man not as an animal but as an organism endowed with a higher mentality. Tylor's definition expressly speaks of " capabilities and habits." But there is a science that deals with capabilities and habits, to wit, psychology. Is it, then, necessary to have a distinct branch of knowledge, or can we not simply merge the cultural phenomena in those of the older science of psychology? It is this question that concerns us here. On the answer must depend our conception of culture and our attitude towards a science purporting to deal with cultural phenomena as something distinct from other data of reality.

In seeking light on this subject we must understand what sort of problems arise from the contemplation of cultural facts and attempt to connect them with the established principles of psychology. A few concrete examples will illustrate the situation.

One of the striking characteristics of our civilization, a trait of our material culture that is nevertheless an invaluable, nay indispensable, means for the propagation of knowledge under modern conditions, is the existence of paper, that is, of a cheap, readily manufactured material for writing and printing. The obvious problem that develops from this fact is, How did we get the art of paper-manufacture? Now we shall search in vain our psychological literature in quest of an explanation. Hoffding and James, Wundt and Titchener have no answer to offer. An answer, nevertheless, exists. Europe learned the art of paper-making from the Arabs, who as early as 795 A.D. had established a paper factory in Bagdad. These in turn got their knowledge from the Chinese, who must be regarded as the originators of the technique. The answer is a perfectly satisfactory one, but it is obviously not couched in psychological terms: its nature is purely historical.

Nevertheless, an objection may plausibly be raised here. Though an explanation has certainly been given, it does not account for all aspects of the phenomena we are considering. There is a psychological basis for each and every one of the events in our historical series. This series we may subdivide into three stages — the invention by the Chinese, the borrowing of this invention by the Arabs, and its transmission from Arab to European. Now the two last-named processes of transmission may not suggest the necessity of a special explanation at all. One may think that all that was required was for the Europeans to watch the Arabs ana for the Arabs to watch the Chinese, and presto! the thing was done. This, indeed, seems to be the view of an influential school of modern ethnologists. But the case is far from being so simple. We know of many instances, in the higher no less than in the lower cultures, corresponding to what the biologist calls symbiosis — a condition where distinct communities or countries persist in a division of labor for mutual benefit, each trading some of its intellectual or material products for equivalents secured from the other. In many parts of Africa there are fixed markets in which negroes from fairly remote localities congregate for the barter of wares, which are thus diffused far from their source of origin; but it is the finished products, not the arts, that are diffused. In New Guinea trading-vessels carry such objects as pottery hundreds of miles from the area of manufacture to natives who remain as ignorant of the ceramic technique as before. In northern Arizona the Hopi Indians occupying three eminences not more than eight miles from one another have no perfect uniformity of industrial knowledge. Pottery,which flourishes on the eastern Mesa, is wholly unknown as an art, though constantly used in its specimens, by the people of the central Mesa; a certain type of basketry plaque is made only at Oraibi village; another type is manufactured exclusively on the central Mesa. Conditions more ideal *a priori* for a transfer of knowledge than among the practically homogeneous neighboring Hopi groups could not be conceived. Nevertheless, it has not taken place. Cultural diffusion, therefore, cannot be taken for granted. We cannot take one people, place it alongside of another, and effect a cultural osmosis in the same way in which we produce a chemical reaction when two substances are brought together under proper conditions of temperature. We are face to face with a selective, with a *psychological* condition. But when we turn once more to our text-books of psychology, we again find nothing that fits the case. About choice in general we get ample information. But we may rummage all the psychological seminar rooms in the world and yet shall find no reason why the Arabs learned the technique of paper-making from the Chinese instead of ignoring it or only importing Chinese paper.

Nor are we more fortunate when we turn to psychology for an account of how the original Chinese inventor came to conceive his epoch-making idea. This fact, of course, falls under the heading of " imagination," and about imagination psychologists have much to tell us. But what, after all, does their interpretation amount to? We learn that imagination, as distinguished from the power of abstract thought, is the power of forming new concrete ideas. Since even the concrete individual idea is complex, being a product of association, its elements may be linked differently so as to produce new combinations. " The inventor of a new mechanism," says Hoffding, " combines given elements, the laws of whose activity he knows, into a totality and a connection which has no complete parallel in experience. "The scientist tries all possible combinations among his elements of experiences, forming a succession of individual ideas, which are rejected until the one appears that adequately represents reality.

We need hardly go farther to realize the impotence of psychological science for illuminating the psychology as well as the history of the paper-making art. The formulation of psychological science is admirable, but it is too general. It explains the invention of the steam-engine and the phonograph, the sewing-machine and the harvester no less than the origin of paper-making. We, however, want to know not merely what ultimate psychological processes the invention of paper-making shares with all other inventions whatsoever, but also the differential conditions that produced this one and unique result under the given circumstances. It is as though we asked about a man's character and were told that he was a vertebrate. The type of psychological explanation we want is by no means unknown; however, we shall find its illustrations not in text-books of psychology, but in histories of literature, science and art. When Taine raises the question how such a bore as Dr. Samuel Johnson could conceivably have attained his position in English literature and answers that it is because of the English predilection , for sermons, he is giving the type of solution — whether right or wrong — that we want to secure for our cultural problem; it explains why the average Englishman, as a member of English society, acquires the habit of regarding Johnson in a certain way. When we inquire why Newton closes his treatise on optics with a statement as to the vanity of human things, our curiosity is satisfied when this expression appears as only one instance of the blending of theological and scientific thought current in his day. It is nonsense to say that these explanations are purely historical; they are psychological, for they take fully into account the subjective attitudes involved in the phenomena studied; and it is "hopeless to expect this sort of explanation from psychological science, which deals with a quite distinct and far more generalized form of mental activity.

Let us turn from the technique of paper manufacture to a different , cultural feature in order to test the possibility of merging the observed phenomena in the principles of psychology. In several parts of the globe, ! and most prominently in parts of South America, the aborigines practise a custom known as the " couvade," which forces the father of a newborn child to subject himself to a period of inactive confinement and a series of rigorously observed dietary and other regulations. Let us, for the sake of bringing out the point in high relief, ignore all historical considerations and concentrate exclusively on the subjective elements involved. Whence, then, this strange and wholly irrational association of ideas between fatherhood and a group of taboos? Now the subject of the association of ideas occupies hundreds of pages in psychological literature, yet all this in itself valuable enough, material has no bearing on our problem, because it is again far too general. We do not doubt for a moment that the association we desire to have illuminated is due either to contiguity or to a perceived similarity of ideas, but why have we this particular association instead of the limitless multitude of associations that would be equally intelligible by the same formulae?

Again, many aboriginal tribes of Australia are subdivided into two halves, membership in which is inherited through the father, in some cases, through the mother in others. These moieties are what is technically called "exogamous," i.e., marriage with a fellow-member is strictly forbidden. The regulation is, indeed, so stringent, the feeling of horror evoked by a transgression so violent, that in former times offenders were promptly put to death. This sentiment is so strong that even when visiting a remote tribe, perhaps a hundred miles away, where there is no possibility of blood-kinship, an Australian will avoidmarriage with a member of the moiety bearing the same name as his own. Here, surely, there is matter for psychology. An Australian has a violent emotional reaction akin to our aversion to incest, and may translate his feelings into the most violent action. Or, looking at the matter from another angle, the Australian exercises an admirable self-control, eschewing on principle marital relations with half the women of his community. Yet all that psychologists tell us of the ethical feelings and the will leaves the problem before us wholly untouched. Why this particular curious feeling developed, what place it occupies in mental life, the psychologist fails to explain. We get, again, simply general formulae about feeling and will that are equally applicable to the case of a man's beating his wife or of a boy's resisting the temptations of a lollypop. And this, it must be noted, is dealing with the distinctively psychological aspect of the data. Whether the rule in question originated in a common center and thence spread to other tribes is also a cultural question of great importance, and this historical phase of the subject psychology is avowedly incompetent to deal with. Psychology, then, fails throughout to supply us with the interpretation we want. It is as impotent to reduce to really interpretative psychological principles the subjective aspect of cultural phenomena as it is to explain the historical sequence of events.

It is not necessary to multiply examples to establish the point. It is clear that cultural phenomena contain elements that cannot be reduced to psychological principles. The reason for the insufficiency is already embodied in Tylor'g definition of culture as embracing " capabilities and habits acquired by man as a member of society." The science of psychology, even in its most modern ramifications of abnormal psychology and the study of individual variations, does not grapple with acquired mental traits, nor with the influence of society on individual thought, feeling and will. It deals, on principle, exclusively with innate traits of the individual. Now, whether the sharp separation assumed here between the innate and the acquired, between individual activity as determined by uniquely individual potentialities and as determined by social environment, can be made in practice or not, one thing is clear: there are phenomena that are acquired and in no sense innate, that are socially and not individually determined. When a Christian reacts in a definite way to the perception of a cross, it is clearly not because of an individual psychic peculiarity, for other

Christians react in the same way. On the other hand, we are not dealing with a general human trait, since the reactions of a Mohammedan or a Buddhist will be quite different. Innumerable instances of this sort show that individual thought, feeling and volition are co-determined by social influences. In so far forth as the potency of these social factors extends we have culture ; in so far forth as knowledge, emotion, and will are neither the result of natural endowment shared with other members of the species nor rest on an individual organic basis, we have a thing *sui generis* that demands for its investigation a distinct science.

Does it follow from the foregoing that there is no possible relation between psychology and culture, that psychological results are a matter of utter indifference to the ethnologist? In their desire to vindicate for their own branch of knowledge a place in the sun, some ethnologists have come very near, if they have not actually reached such a conclusion To me the case appears in a somewhat different light. Whatever division of labor may be desirable for the economy of scientific work, knowledge as a whole knows nothing of watertight compartments. Further, the nominally distinct sciences are not subordinated to one another, but coexist in a condition of democratic equality and coopera-tiveness. We cannot reduce cultural to psychological phenomena any more than we can reduce biology to mechanics or chemistry, because in either case the very facts we desire to have explained are ignored in the more generalized formulation. But for specific purposes, the student of culture can call for aid upon each and all of the other branches of learning. It is a very important cultural problem whether the natives of South America knew the bronze technique, i.e., whether they consciously produced the observed alloy of copper and tin. But how can the ethnologist solve this problem? Only by requisitioning the services of the chemist.

Now very few would deny that services of the kind

rendered by chemistry can also be rendered to the study of culture by psychology. Indeed, most people would at once admit that the relationship with psychology is *a priori* likely to be far more extensive and thoroughgoing. A few concrete examples will illustrate how this relationship may be conceived.

Among the quaint conceits with which primitive cultures abound is that of attaching to particular numbers a peculiar character of sanctity " Everything in the universe," a Crow Indian once told me, " goes by fours." As a matter of fact, most things in Crow religious life are adjusted to this conception. An important ceremonial act is thrice feigned so as to be actually performed at the fourth attempt; religious processions halt four times; songs are sung in sets of four; in mythic tales it is the fourth trial that carries an heroic feat to a successful issue. Now this cultural fact very largely eludes psychological interpretation. The first thing that strikes us is that this feature is no peculiarity of the Crow, but is rather widely distributed among their immediate neighbors and even remote Indian tribes, though jointly occupying a continuous area. Since outside of this region other numbers figure as mystic, we cannot regard the view of the sacredness of Four as a general trait of human psychology but must assume that the concept was borrowed by most of the tribes now holding it. A wider survey teaches us that corresponding, though not identical, conceptions are very common.*Seven* figures in parts of Asia, *Three* in European folklore, *Five* in Oregon and northern Nevada, *Six* among the Ainu of Yezo, *Nine* among the Yakut, *Ten* among the Pythagorean philosophers of ancient Greece, very much as *Four* does among the Crow. Now the fact that a particular Crow Indian regards Four as a sacred number does not mean that this is an individual peculiarity of his any more than the Christian's reaction to a cross is a proof of some psychological idiosyncrasy. Individually the Crow Indian may be quite indifferent to the number and yet he would view it as sacred because he has been taught so to regard it. This is, of course, the vital difference between ethnology and psychology which has already been emphasized. Nevertheless, the association must at one time have been formed in an individual mind whether among the Crow or elsewhere, and the question arises as to what such an association means. Francis Galton showed some time ago that such associations of definite personal characteristics with numbers occur by no means infrequently among Europeans. The phenomenon we are dealing with is thus linked with a group of related phenomena and in so far forth is explained.

There are ethnologists who would not admit that such an explanation has anything to do with ethnology. They would contend that as soon as we cease to investigate the group as such we are passing from ethnology, the science of culture, to psychology, the science of individual minds. This seems an unnecessarily narrow doctrinaire view. Knowledge, as stated above, is not sub-divided by hard-and-fast partitions. Interest certainly does not stop at an arbitrary point in the investigation but is centered on a comprehension of the whole phenomenon. Where that phenomenon is an alloy of tin and copper, a decision as to its nature is naturally left to chemistry; it seems not unreasonable that where it is a type of association we should turn for enlightenment to psychology.

Another field supplies an additional illustration. One of the important subjects for ethnographic study is artistic form. The ethnologist notes in a purely descriptive way the decorative patterns employed by various tribes, the fact that curvilinear motives are prominent among the Maori of New Zealand while the rawhide bags of Plains Indians are covered with angular paintings. Here, once more, it is clear that many of the problems that arise are purely cultural. There are, nevertheless, psychological elements involved that may be misunderstood without psychological knowledge. Let us assume, e.g., that a certain tribe is artistically characterized by a fondness for squares. What does this predilection signify? It is a psychological commonplace that through an optical illusion we exaggerate the height as compared with the width of a rectangle; accordingly, the geometrical square does not coincide with the psychological square. This simple piece of information enables us to understand what we are actually dealing with in the case of a square pattern. At the same time it sharpens our observation regarding such patterns. It is quite conceivable that in one place tribal taste should prefer the actual square while elsewhere the psychological square occupies the seat of honor. This would be a purely ethnographic fact, yet its discovery might be considerably expedited by some knowledge of experimental aesthetics.

Let us turn from mystic numbers and decorative designs to another aspect of primitive life. The Turkish tribes of western Siberia have a form of religion based on the belief that certain individuals enjoy the hereditary privilege of acting as intermediaries between their ancestral spirits and the people at large. With the aid of his sacred drum the shaman, as such an intermediary is technically called, is able to summon the supernatural beings, cure the sick, foretell the future, separate his own soul from his body and send it to the upper realms of light or the nether regions of darkness. Now, although a particular individual inherits the shaman's office from his father, he receives no formal instructions nor does he make any active preparation for his mission. His call comes in the form of a sudden paroxysm. He is seized with a feeling of languor and a fit of violent convulsions, with abnormal yawning and a powerful pressure on the chest, which cause him to utter inarticulate screams. He begins to shiver with cold, rolls his eyes, suddenly leaps up and madly circles about until he falls down covered with perspiration and writhing in epileptic spasms on the ground. His members are devoid of sensation, his hands grasp without discrimination red-hot iron, knives, pins; he swallows such objects without suffering the slightest injury, and again ejects them from his mouth. Finally, the prospective seer seizes a shaman's drum and assumes the shaman's office. Disobedience to the spirit's call would spell disaster, madness and death amidst the most horrible tortures.

The naive reaction to this narrative on the part of common sense in the familiar form of common ignorance will probably be that the European traveler who is our authority is a very gullible individual if he believed his native informant's statements. How can an individual be seized with such a spasm as that described? How is it possible for him to become devoid of sensation? Nevertheless, nothing is more certain than that the account given is substantially correct. It is simply a particular form of nervous affliction very common throughout Siberia and attested by dozens of trustworthy eyewitnesses. This Arctic hysteria, as it has been misnamed (for there is nothing distinctively Arctic about it), manifests itself principally in two ways. Either the individual falls victim to an indiscriminate mania for mimicking the acts of others; or he is seized with the sort of paroxysm described for the Turkish shaman. Nothing is clearer than that in neither case is there usually conscious deception. Sometimes the imitation mania subjects the sufferer to ridicule and pain, as when an old woman in imitation of a Cossack, seized a salmon with her teeth, ran up a hill and down again, unable to prevent herself from plunging into the water, though normally she was barely able to walk. Similarly, the numerous hysterical individuals of the other type who do not become inspired shamans cannot possibly derive any benefit from their fits.

Abnormal psychology here steps in and teaches us that such trances are involuntary and not the result of fraud, that they occur in our own civilization and are accompanied with extraordinary lack of sensibility to pain, in short, psychiatry classifies the observed phenomena and tells us what we are really dealing with. It prevents a misconception alike of the shaman's activities and of the attitude of his people towards him.

When, however, abnormal psychology has so far enlightened us, it has by no means exhausted even the purely subjective aspect of the case. How does the prospective shaman seized with his fit know about the shamanistic drum that forms a necessary accessory of his office? How does he know what mode of activity is expected from him? These are not things which he can get directly from his trance, for we shall hardly accept the aboriginal theory that he is inspired by the ancestral spirits. He can derive his knowledge, however informally, only as the member of a group holding certain definite views as to the shamanistic office. The cultural phenomenon, then, even on its psychological side, comprises a very appreciable *plus* over and above the facts that psychology can explain, and these additional data accordingly require treatment by another science.

My conclusions as to the relation of psychology to culture are, accordingly, the following: The cultural facts, even in their subjective aspect, are not merged in psychological facts. They must not, indeed, contravene psychological principles, but the same applies to all other principles of the universe; culture cannot construct houses contrary to the laws of gravitation nor produce bread out of stones. But the principles of psychology are as incapable of accounting tor the phenomena of culture as is gravitation to account for architectural styles. Over and above the interpretations given by psychology, there is an irreducible residuum of huge magnitude that calls for special treatment and by its very existence vindicates the *raison d'etre* of ethnology. We need not eschew any help given by scientific psychology for the comprehension of specifically psychological components of cultural phenomena; but as no one dreams of saying that these phenomena are reduced to chemical principles when chemistry furnishes us with an analysis of Peruvian bronze implements, so no one can dare assert that they are reduced to psychological principles when we call upon psychology to elucidate specific features of cultural complexes. The " capabilities and habits acquired by man as a member of society " constitute a distinct aspect of reality that must be the field of a distinct science autonomous with reference to psychology.

THE SUBTLENESS OF CULTURAL INFLUENCES

The educated cosmopolite does not hesitate to try strange foods. Not so the savage, the child and the ignorant. In these three classes, food prejudices_often curious and irrational — abound. In California, a man and woman sitting near me in the car expressed great curiosity about the immense fields of blue-green French artichokes. I explained what these vegetables were, how they were served and eaten, dwelt on their toothsomeness and recommended a trial. " Oh, no! " said the man, with the utmost finality, " We never eat strange foods."

Here spoke the cosmopolite's " contemporary ancestor." In a hostile world the savage must take heed what he eats or he may rue the day. Although many of his food taboos are doubtless fanciful, others are ' based on substantial reasons. One of his remote ancestors may have experimented with a strange food and was poisoned by it, and the tradition has become fixed in the tribe. An overripe oyster may cause death, while venison, aged in the cache, may be a nourishing delicacy. His tribe for generations has known what foods are good and he avoids all others — all " strange foods." Food prejudices to-day, therefore, are due to inheritance from our savage ancestry; they are atavistic.

On both the American and European shores of the Atlantic Ocean two shellfish are common, the soft-shelled clam, *Mya arenaria*, and the edible mussel, *Mytilus edulis*. The species of these two mollusks are the same on both sides of the water. In Europe, mussels are eaten freely but not clams, while the reverse is the case on the American side. This prejudice, against the mussel here and against the clam there, extends back to prehistoric times, for while clam shells abound here in kitchen middens or ancient shell heaps and mussel shells are merely accidental, in Europe the exact opposite is the case.

Professor Edward S. Morse, in his study of the changes in the shell of the clam (*Scientific Monthly*, xxi, 1925, p. 424), was amazed to find no clam shells in the Baltic shell heaps, while the living mollusks abounded in the nearby estuaries. The prehistoric people like their modern successors did not eat the clam. He adds: " It was the same in England; the clam had never been eaten, even in ancient times. It is a common shell there, and thousands of barrels are shipped to the Newfoundland fisheries for bait. We learned the epicurean delights of the clam from the North American Indians." In a recent visit on the Norfolk coast of England I had great difficulty in persuading a company of educated English people to taste the clam!

Children are nearer the savage state, more atavistic than their educated parents, and strange foods are often to them abominations. The wise parent instils the precept, " Eat what is set before you and be thankful," and, to take the sting off, he may add, with a twinkle in his eye, " put your food into your mouth and not into your lap." The unwise parent allows the innate talent for food prejudices to grow strong in his young hopefuls, and even boasts that his little Johnny or Mary can not eat this and can not eat that. I do not refer here to certain rare idiosyncrasies, as, for example, when even a minute amount of egg causes symptoms of poisoning, for that fortunately does not often happen to Johnny and Mary, and they have no inborn prejudices which warn them against such food. Food prejudices run rife among them. It may be observed, as in the case of the travelers and the French artichoke, that the victim does not even taste the food that falls under his taboo. His mind is made up without that. He *knows* the food is not fit for him to eat, and the fact that others eat it and enjoy it and thrive makes no difference.

The third class mentioned above, the ignorant, is well represented — or rather used to be — by the peasant servant girl who was content with corned beef and cabbage, and refused even to taste venison and wild duck.

All of us are very near the savage state, for our civilized ancestry is but a minute fraction of our whole human ancestry. Food prejudices, therefore, abound even among the educated. In the matter of fish, this is strikingly the case. In England and in this country the various kinds of flatfish, whether known as sole, plaice or flounder, are considered good and delicate eating and bring a high price either in the market or restaurant. This is not the case in the Gaspe Peninsula, in Newfoundland and in Labrador. In Newfoundland I once read an editorial in a St. John's paper urging the use of this fish as a food and recounting the fact — singular to Newfoundlanders — that the flounder brought high prices in the States. At Grand Greve in Gaspesia I told a fisherman and his wife, at whose house I was staying, the high esteem and high price in which the flounder was held in Boston, and suggested that the next he caught should not be wasted. I am afraid I damaged my reputation for truthfulness by mentioning the price. A few days later I saw several flounders deposited as fertilizer in the garden, and, on my exclaiming at the sacrilege, he said," Oh, they are not fit to eat! " There was nothing more to be said.

In my youth, when on codfishing excursions I caught pollack, no matter how large and fine, I was told to return them to the water as they were " not fit to eat." Nowadays this prejudice seems to have disappeared. At Grand Manan, New Brunswick, haddock and hake were formerly thrown away, and nearly everywhere along our coasts the dogfish, hated by fishermen for the damage it does to fish and nets and bait, is destroyed and cast out. It is true that it has an unpleasant name for a food fish — for there is much in a name, Shakespeare to the contrary notwithstanding — and it is also true that the dogfish is a shark, but let me add that it has firm white flesh which is nearly as good eating as that of the esteemed swordfish. The first time that I determined to try the gastronomic qualities of this fish and had expected to be obliged to prepare and cook it myself, I was agreeably surprised to find that our cook, a native of the Hebrides, welcomed it as an old friend and prepared a savory dish of it. For some reason the inhabitants of the Hebrides, or at least of that part from which she came, had no prejudices against the dogfish. To avoid this prejudice, the names " gray fish " and "rock salmon " are used here and in England.

It may be thought that the knowledge of the food on which the fish or other creatures live has a great deal to do with food prejudices, but when we consider the food of the domestic hen and of the domestic pig, it is hard to conceive of anything worse. Make no inquiry as to the food of the lobster!

Norman Heathcote, in " Birds of St. Kilda," says that the favorite dish at this island was " skate which was beginning to go bad." Parenthetically, I might remark that we prefer our game " when it is beginning to go bad," and I might add that the skate like the dogfish is a kind of shark.

In Labrador, young gulls are considered great delicacies as food, while the mere idea of eating cormorants is a thing abhorrent, yet gulls feed on the flotsam and jetsam of the sea, on long-dead fish as well as on fresh ones.

Cormorants, on the other hand, feed exclusively on freshly caught fish. On a cruise along the Labrador coast I once broiled the breast of one of these birds. The two sailors turned away from it in horror — I had not been able to persuade one of them, the cook, to prepare it — but the captain, a broad-minded man and one who could rise above prejudices, much to his surprise, found it delicious, as, indeed, it was. It is possible that the uncanny neck of this bird with the bare patch of orange-colored skin at the throat has something to do with the prejudice, but no one objects to the turkey, which has a still more uncanny head and neck.

To " eat crow " has an unpleasant metaphorical flavor. Equally unpleasant, even abhorrent to most people, is the idea of eating crow in the literal sense. The crow stands at the head of the bird world in brain capacity. He has no food prejudices, but his bill of fare is dainty compared with that of the barnyard fowl. Now I can assert that a properly broiled or roasted crow, especially if young, compares well with pigeon or squab. Very few, I am convinced, would approach the subject with an unprejudiced mind or palate, so that, no doubt, the experiment would fail, to my discomfiture, but I can add that I have found some to agree with me. Fair judgment in such matters is difficult or impossible to the victim of food prejudices. It is conceivable that honey might taste to him like vinegar. Rook shooting and rook eating in Pickwick's time, at least, was common sport in England. A rook is a crow.

I remember reading a sportsman's recipe for cooking porcupine which included long stewings and changes of water. The recipe concluded with the advice — which was excellent under the circumstances — to throw it all away without serving. A nicely broiled porcupine steak or hind quarter, I can, however, aver from experience, to be excellent. The same can be said of woodchuck, muskrat and skunk; I have tried them all. Indians are particularly fond of skunk, which, be it added, is known in the Algonquin tongue as *shikago* [Chicago] — tell it not in Gath!

Explorers in savage regions often learn to divest themselves of food prejudices. Captain G. F. Lyon, of H. M. S. *Hecla,* in a voyage of discovery in the Arctic regions under Captain Parry, was a good example. He says, " All were horrified at the idea of eating foxes, but very many got the better of their delicacy and found them good eating. Not being myself very nice, I soon made the experiment, and found the flesh much resembling that of kid, and afterwards frequently had a supper of it."

Captain George Cartwright, who lived from 1770 to 1786 on the Lab-rador coast, was another such adventurous soul. He found his men re-belled at being made to eat venison in winter in order to conserve the salt pork which they preferred, and only by an artifice did he get them to eat polar bear.

Stefansson, in " The Friendly Arctic," gives a very good account of food prejudices among Esquimaux dogs. He found that the dogs brought up far from the sea and fed on caribou and rabbit would not eat seal meat, while those brought up on the seashore and used to seal meat would not touch other game when they were taken inland. He found that in young dogs the prejudice was more quickly overcome than in old dogs who would sometimes endure starvation rather than try the new food, and that old females were the most obstinate in refusing to give up their prejudices. This leads him to conclude — rather ungallantly, perhaps — that " this seems to extend the commonly believed-in principle of the greater conservatism of human females down into the lower animals." The highly civilized dog, used to all kinds of foods, has, as is obvious, few or no food prejudices.

It is well known that the introduction of potatoes and tomatoes in Europe was a slow and difficult process, and that Indian corn meal is even now considered fit only for poultry in most parts of the British Isles, while the introduction of grapefruit as a part of the breakfast ritual has met with considerable opposition. In Labrador, turnip greens are eaten, but beet greens are thrown away.

Food prejudices are not limited to the savage, the child and the ignorant. They are found even among the intelligent and educated. An extreme case I discovered recently in an intelligent and educated man over threescore years of age. He admitted that he was much Spoiled as a child and that until he was twenty-one he had refused to taste any vegetable but the potato. After this he gradually overcame many of his vegetable prejudices, but he still refuses to eat or even taste beets. The reason he can not give unless it be its color, but he admits that this is unreasonable, for he is very fond of strawberries. Of banana, watermelon and cantaloupe he has never even tasted, and he shudders to think of trying them. Although he lives in the pie belt and is fond of apple pie, he can pot bring himself to try squash or pumpkin pie. How many good things in life this man has missed owing to his treasured food prejudices! How much better for him had he been brought up to eat the food set before him and be thankful, even if he did put some of the food into his lap!

CULTURAL AND PSYCHOLOGICAL DIFFERENCES

It is customary to speak of the customs and thought prevailing among a people as their culture. Since, in all cultural activities, ideas and judgments play important parts, it has often been assumed that a detailed comparison of cultures would reveal psychological differences between the peoples to whom the cultures belonged.

Indeed, some persons go so far as to assert that the existence of cultural differences necessitates the existence of psychological differences. Yet when the subject is taken on its merits, several difficulties are encountered. In the first place, some definite method of grading cultures must be devised before satisfactory conclusions as to corresponding psychological differences can be formed. As yet, no consistent way of grading as to higher or lower has been found.

Further, anthropologists now believe in the existence of a tendency to conventionalize thought and the association of ideas as a factor in the differentiation of culture. Such a tendency appears when the symbolic art of such tribes as the Arapaho, Dakota, and Shoshoni are compared, each using similar designs, but associated with different kinds of ideas. Also, some claim has been made, but on less definite grounds, that Indian mythology as a whole is less closely associated with creators and gods than is the case with other peoples. In a more general way, we find everywhere among the Indians a marked tendency to interassociate the sociological, religious, and artistic aspects of their lives to such a degree that they can scarcely be unraveled.

This has sometimes been taken as one of the most characteristic aspects of Indian modes of thought. The claim is made, however, that such conventions of thought can not in themselves be taken as indications of functional differences between minds (as such) of Indians and other races; since, on *a priori* grounds, what has become conventional or habitual for one may in turn become conventional for another.

This theory, that all cultural differences are in no wise due to psychological differences, but to causes entirely external, or outside of the conscious life, places the innerent worth of a Pigmy, an Indian, a Mongol, and a European upon the same level, and considers culture as the sum of the habits into which the various groups of mankind have fallen. While strong arguments in support of this interpretation of culture are offered by many anthropologists, together with plausible reasons for doubting the existence of fundamental psychological differences in function, so far nothing has been brought forward to ender doubtful the existence of psychological differences between aces analogous to those between individuals among ourselves.

CULTURE AND MENTAL PROCESSES : CONTEMPORARY TOTEMISM

Many modern anthropologists discount the supposed differences in the mental processes of civilized and uncivilized peoples and hold that the psychological factors which have controlled the growth of the so-called primitive cultures are still at work in modern society. It is difficult to obtain evidence on this point, and a record of the development in the American army of a series of beliefs and practices which show a considerable resemblance to the totemic complexes existing among some primitive peoples may, therefore, be of interest. The growth of one of these pseudo-totemic complexes can be fully traced in the case of the 42nd or Rainbow Division. The name was arbitrarily chosen by the higher officials and is said to have been selected because the organization was made up of units from many states whose regimental colors were of every hue in the rainbow. Little importance was attached to the name while the division was in America and it was rarely used by enlisted men. After the organization arrived in France, its use became increasingly common, and the growth of a feeling of divisional solidarity finally resulted in its regular employment as a personal appellation. Outsiders usually addressed division members as " Rainbow," and to the question " What are you? " nine out of ten enlisted men would reply " I'm a Rainbow." This personal use of the name became general before any attitude toward the actual rainbow was developed. A feeling of connection between the organization and its namesake was first noted in February, 1918, five to six months after the assignment of the name. At this time it was first suggested and then believed that the appearance of a rainbow was a good omen for the division. Three months later it had become an article of faith in the organization that there was always a rainbow in the sky when the division went into action. A rainbow over the enemy's lines was considered especially auspicious, and after a victory men would often insist that they had seen one in this position even when the weather conditions or direction of advance made it impossible. This belief was held by most of the officers and enlisted men, and anyone who expressed doubts was considered a heretic and overwhelmed with arguments.

The personal use of the divisional name and the attitude toward the rainbow had both become thoroughly established before it began to be used as an emblem. In the author's regiment this phase first appeared in May, when the organization came in contact with the 77th Division which had its namesake, the Goddess of Liberty, painted on its carts and other divisional property. The idea was taken up at once, and many of the men decorated the carts and limbers in their charge with rainbows without waiting for official permission. As no two of the painted rainbows were alike, the effect was grotesque and the practice was soon forbidden. Nevertheless it continued, more or less surreptitiously, until after the armistice, when it was finally permitted with a standardized rainbow.

The use of rainbows as personal insignia appeared still later, in August or September. The history of the development of shoulder insignia in the American Army is well known and need not be given here. The idea apparently originated with the Canadian forces, but the "A. E. F. received it indirectly through one of the later American organizations which had adopted it before their arrival in France. The use of such insignia became general in the rear areas before it reached the divisions at the front. The first shoulder insignia seen by the author's regiment were worn by a salvage corps and by one of the newer divisions. This division was rumored to have been routed in its first battle, and it was believed that its members were forced to wear the insignia as punishment. The idea thus reached the 42nd Division under unfavorable auspices, but it was immediately taken up and passed through nearly the same phases as the use of painted insignia on divisional property. The wearing of shoulder insignia was at first forbidden by some of the regimental commanders, but even while it was proscribed many of the men carried insignia with them and pinned them on whenever they were out of reach of their officers. They were worn by practically all members of the division when in the rear areas, and their use by outsiders or even by the men sent to the division as replacements, was resented and punished. In the case of replacements, the stricture was relaxed as they became recognized members of the group.

All the other army organizations which were in existence long enough to develop a feeling of group solidarity seem to have built up similar complexes centering about their group names. The nature of some of these names precluded the development of the ideas of the namesake's guardianship or omen giving, but in such cases the beliefs which were associated with the rainbow by the 42nd Division were usually developed in connection with something other than the group namesake. In some organizations the behavior of an animal mascot, or even of an abnormal person, was considered ominous. In one instance a subnormal hysteric acquired a reputation as a soothsayer and was relieved of regular duty by the other enlisted men on condition that he foretell the outcome of an expected attack. The successive stages in the development of these complexes were not always the same as in the case of the 42nd Division. Many of the later organizations seem to have taken over such complexes with little change except the substitution of their namesake for that of the group from which they borrowed.

By the end of the war, the A. E. F. had become organized

into a series of well defined, and often mutually jealous, groups each of which had its individual complex of ideas and observances. These complexes all conformed to the same general pattern but differed in content. The individual complexes bound the members of each group together and enabled them to present a united front against other groups. In the same way the uniformity of pattern gave a basis for mutual understanding and tolerance and united all the groups against persons or organizations outside the system.

The conditions in the American army after these group complexes had become fully developed may be summarized as follows:

1. A division of the personnel into a number of groups conscious of their individuality;
2. the possession by each of these groups of a distinctive name derived from some animal, object or natural phenomenon;
3. the use of this name as a personal appellation in conversation with outsiders;
4. the use of representations of the group namesake for the decoration of group property and for personal adornment, with a taboo against its use by members of other groups;
5. a reverential attitude toward the group namesake and its representations ;
6. in many cases, an unformulated belief that the group namesake was also a group guardian capable of giving omens.

Almost any investigator who found such a condition existing among an uncivilized people would class these associated beliefs and practices as a totemic complex. It shows a poverty of content when contrasted with the highly developed totemism of the Australians or Melanesians, but is fully as rich as the totemic complexes of some of the North

American Indian tribes. The main points in which it differs from true totemism are the absence of marriage regulations, of beliefs in descent from, or of blood relationship with, the totem, and of special rites or observances to propitiate the totem. Each of these features is lacking in one or another of the primitive complexes which are usually classed as totemic and one of the most important, marriage regulation, is clearly a function of the clan or gentile system of organization and occurs in primitive groups for which totemism can not be proved.

It seems probable that both the A. E. F. complexes and primitive totemism are results of the same social and supernaturalistic tendencies. The differences in the working out of these tendencies can readily be accounted for by the differences in the framework to which they have attached themselves and in the cultural patterns which have shaped their expression. In the army, the military unit offered a crystallization point for these tendencies, and this precluded the development of marriage regulations or of a belief in the common ancestry of the group. The American culture pattern stimulated the development of the eponymous and decorative features, but offered no formulae for the rationalization of the relation felt to exist between the group and is namesake, or for the development of observances for the namesake's propitiation. In primitive groups, on the other hand, the same tendencies usually crystallized about a clan or gentile system, and the marriage regulation features of this system become incorporated into the complex. Membership in the clan or gens was based on common descent, and in a group which drew no clear line between mankind and the rest of nature, the idea of blood relationship provided a convenient formula for the explanation of the group-namesake relation. Animistic or polytheistic concepts, and the existence of observances for the propitiation of a number of supernatural beings, afforded a pattern for the development of religious attitudes and special observances in connection with the namesake.

Even if we are willing to admit the essential unity of the tendencies which produced the army complexes on one hand and the totemic complexes on the other, it does not follow that the observed development of the army complexes will throw much light on the history of primitive totemism. Even in the army no universal rule of evolution was evident, for although the starting-points were always the group and name, the other features appeared in different order in the various units. The ease and rapidity with which the army complexes were developed suggests that the tendencies underlying them were deep-seated and only awaited a chance for expression. The importance of diffusion in the growth of these complexes is suggestive, and the army conditions may afford a clue to the true significance of some totemic phenomena. The often quoted example of the Australian who declared he was a kangaroo is a case in point. The author repeatedly heard soldiers declare that they were sunsets, wild cats, etc., and it would have required a good deal of questioning to obtain any coherent explanation of the relation which they felt existed between themselves and their namesakes. Such a cross-examination would have been impossible with the limited vocabulary of a trade jargon and very difficult with an ordinary interpreter. Although the army attitudes and practices were definite enough, their background was emotional rather than rational and the average soldier never attempted to formulate the ideas underlying them. Explanations elicited by questioning would be made up on the spur of the moment and would represent only his individual opinion. It seems probable that in primitive groups also a whole series of attitudes and practices could be developed without the individual feeling any need for their rationalization until he was confronted by some anthropological investigator.

CULTURE AND MENTAL PROCESSES : THE RISE OF A TABOO

To expose the origin of a social taboo is to reveal an important factor in social control. It is the purpose of this paper to trace the rise of a group taboo in a pioneer society in western America. The particular example will be that of the rise of the taboo on the killing of a gull among the Mormons in the early days of their settlement in Utah.

The first group of Mormons, 143 in number, arrived in the valley of the Great Salt Lake on July 24, 1847. Some small tracts of land were put under irrigation within a few weeks. Throughout the summer additional " companies " of pioneers arrived and before autumn considerable land was brought under cultivation. By the spring of 1848, the colony was fairly well established. Whitney, in his " History of Utah," describes the situation as follows:

The opening of the spring of 1848 in Great Salt Lake City saw nearly seventeen hundred souls dwelling in upwards of four hundred log and adobe huts inside the " Old Fort." Over five thousand acres of land had been brought under cultivation, nearly nine hundred acres of which had been sown with winter wheat, the tender blades of which were now beginning to sprout.

Naturally the strain on the food supply had been very severe during the winter of 1847-1848 and the settlers were thoroughly dependent for survival upon the forthcoming harvest of 1848. Their remoteness from outside sources of food supply was obvious. And during the summer of 1848 hundreds more of Mormons arrived from the Missouri River region, which but added to the demands on the food resources for the coming winter.

In May and June of 1848 large numbers of crickets *(Anabrus simplex)* began to appear in the wheat fields. At first little attention was paid to these pests, but as time went on they increased in number and in the damage they did to the growing crops. Mr. Anson Call, one of the Utah pioneers, gives the following pious but amusing description of the insect:

The Rocky Mountain Cricket, as now remembered, when full grown is about one-and-a-half inches in length, heavy and clumsy in its movements, with no better power of locomotion than hopping a foot or two at a time. It has an eagle-eyed, staring appearance, and suggests the idea that it may be the habitation of a vindictive little demon.

The crickets made another intense crisis for the already much harassed Mormons. Removed both by distance and by prejudice from assistance, the very existence of the group seemed at the time to be threatened. Every effort was made to drive off the pests. Whitney writes of the period:

With the energy of desperation, the community, men, women and children, thoroughly alarmed, marshalled themselves to fight and if possible to repel the rapacious foe. While some went through the fields killing the crickets, and at the same time, alas! crushing much of the tender grain, others dug ditches around the farms, turned water into the ditches, and drove and drowned therein myriads of the black devourers. Others beat them back with clubs and brooms, or burned them in fires set in the fields. Still they could not prevail. Too much headway had been gained by the crickets before the gravity of the situation was discovered, and in spite of all that the settlers could do, their hopes of a harvest were vanishing, and with these hopes the very hope of life.

The pressure of hunger became very real. One of the settlers, Parley P. Pratt, thus describes the hardship of his family:

During this spring and summer my family and myself, in common with many of the camp, suffered much for want of food. . . . We had lost nearly all our cows, and the few which were spared to us were dry. ... I had ploughed and subdued land to the amount of nearly forty acres. ... In this labor every woman and child in my family, so far as they were of sufficient age and strength, had joined to help me, and toiled incessantly in the field, suffering every hardship which human nature could well endure. Myself and some of them were compelled to go with bare feet for several months, reserving our Indian moccasins for extra occasions. We toiled hard and lived on a few greens, and on the thistle and other roots.

The writer has been told by persons who lived through this period that the domestic fowls of the households devoured such quantities of the crickets as to make their eggs quite unpalatable, thus cutting off a minor source of food. Furthermore, the crickets attacked the small grazing lands available for live stock, thus adding another burden to the major one.

Now the nearby Paiute Indians found in these very crickets a pleasant delicacy and ate them in large numbers. But the food-habits of the white man prevented a sensible adaptation to the Indian usage. Differences in culture make differences of tastes.

The Mormons, like all people of primitive culture status, confused natural with supernatural or magical practices. And while they made untiring attempts to combat these pests, they also resorted to prayer and magic for release from the strain and problem. Man confronted with the futility of his own efforts seems to resort to supplication or to magic, or both, to obtain his desires. So, here, entreaties were made for divine intervention to free them from this plague. The followingMormon account gives at once the essential facts of the situation and also the settlers' rationalization of the event:

They were saved, they believed, by a miracle. ... In the

midst of the work of destruction, when it seemed as if nothing could stay the devastation, great flocks of gulls appeared, filling the air with their white wings and plaintive cries, and settled down upon the half-ruined fields. At first it seemed as if they came but to destroy what the crickets had left. But their real purpose was soon apparent. They came to prey upon the destroyers. All day long they gorged themselves, and when full, disgorged and feasted again, the white gulls upon the black crickets, like hosts of heaven and hell contending, until the pests were vanquished, and the people were saved. The heaven-sent birds then returned to the lake islands whence they came, leaving the grateful people to shed tears of joy at the wonderful and timely deliverance wrought out for them.

Bancroft, in his " History of Utah," reports that later in the same season grasshoppers or the " migratory " locusts (*Melanophus spretus*), did considerable damage to the remaining crops. And the next year the crickets appeared again, although not in such numbers. This, coupled with drought and frosts, made the second year almost as severe as the first. From time to time during the next ten years the pioneers had to combat both crickets and grasshoppers. In 1854 and in 1855 the crops failed due to the grasshoppers. This reduced the group to straitened circumstances and in these years the gulls did " not come to the rescue."

Yet for the year 1848 the " miracle " of the gulls meant survival. Naturally much significance was attached to their visitation. The superstitious pioneers gave thanks to their god for deliverance from threatened disaster. The crisis of famine had been met successfully by what seemed divine intervention. The crops were harvested and though not bounteous were sufficient to see them through the coming winter. The harvest festival which was held is typical of a group-response to this happy solution of a serious crisis Bancroft writes:

On the tenth of August, however, the harvest being then gathered, a feast was held in the bowery (a community structure for religious services), at which the tables were loaded with a variety of viands, vegetables, beef, and bread, butter and cheese, with cakes and pastry. Sheaves of wheat and other grain were hoisted on harvest poles; and [says Parley P. Pratt] there was prayer and thanksgiving, congratulations, songs, speeches, music, dancing, smiling faces, and merry hearts. . . .

The Mormons naturally developed a high reverence for the gull. Songs were sung, poems written, sermons and personal " testimonies " given concerning the supernatural deliverance. The bird became a sacred object to these people. The territorial government which was organized shortly thereafter and which was completely Mormon in composition, passed legislation prohibiting the killing of the gull. The official Mormon historian, Mr. Whitney, gives the following panegyric on the birds:

Is it strange that among the early acts of Utah's legislators there should be a law making the wanton killing of these birds a punishable offense? Rome once had her sacred geese. Utah would thenceforth have her sacred gulls. Ye statesmen and state-makers of the future! When Utah's sovereign star, dawning above the dark horizon of factional strife, shall take its place in the blue, unclouded zenith of freedom's empyrean, and it is asked by those who would frame her escutcheon what shall her emblem be? Name not at all the carpetbag Place not first the bee-hive, nor the eagle; not yet the miner's pick, the farmer's plow, nor the smoke-stack of the wealth-producing smelter. Give these their places, all, in dexter or in middle, but whatever else the glittering shield contains, reserve for the honor point, as worthy of all praise, the sacred bird that saved the pioneers.

While the Mormon statesmen did not heed Mr. Whitney's suggestion, the gull incident has continued to play a very large part in the folk-lore and history of the state. And as a final culmination to this development, as an artistic rationalization, has come the erection of the " Sea-gull Monument " in Salt Lake City, showing atop a shaft of thirty feet or so a golden ball upon which two gulls are placed. Around the base of this monument are four reliefs portraying the coming of the pioneers into the Great Basin, the planting of crops, the contest with the crickets and, finally, the " miraculous " deliverance by the gulls.

So much for the story. What as to its meaning for the study of the rise of a social taboo and a folk-lore?

In the first instance, it must be noted that although this religious body drew most of its fundamentals from such creeds as the Campbell-ites, the Baptists and from the general Puritan tradition, its concepts were decidedly primitive throughout. The belief in direct, divine revelation was basic as was the belief in a divinely appointed priesthood and in miracle-working. The long history of hardship and persecution had produced an intense loyalty and sense of social solidarity. The pioneer life had thrown these people into a distinctly alien and elemental country with a reduction of life to a direct struggle for existence. It is true that they brought with them the material culture of their contemporary civilization, which enabled them to till the soil, put irrigation into effect and to construct a more adequate economic life than the Indians around them had. But as to what may be called non-material or psycho-social culture, especially on the side of religious beliefs and notions of magical power and supernatural influences, they were not greatly advanced over the Middle Ages or the peasant peoples of Europe and Asia. As one must recognize at all times, the state of learning and the manner of life are not a matter of time or place but of cultural level. In regard to interpretations of natural phenomena, the Mormons were much inclined to magical thinking.

While their Protestant background prevented the development of a whole seriés of rituals and public festivals in reference to the gulls, certainly a rigid, rather superstitious taboo arose concerning them. Furthermore, the rise of the bird to a position of worship as a totem of the group was incipient but prevented by the existence of other culture patterns of more complex sort drawn from their religious and theological background. Still, we may note, in conclusion, how much of rudimentary reaction and interpretation did remain. We may summarize the following stages in the development of this whole culture complex of the gull:

1. We have a severe group crisis. The food supply is threatened by the pest of crickets. Group survival is at stake.
2. There is an inability to cope with the situation by any naturalistic means. In other words, common-sense techniques do not suffice to allay the crisis.
3. There is a turning to God for help. Actually, of course, with these vigorous people there was a combination of work and prayer. Aggressive Christian peoples facing starvation are not apt to forget the injunction to *faith and works.*
4. There is some delay in the answer to the first entreaties to God for deliverance. Men of that generation of Mormons have been known to say that this occurred " in order to test the faith of the people " — a very typical rationalization. Thus the crisis continues to grow more and more alarming and this in spite of renewed efforts of their own techniques and of additional piety.
5. There is a growing despair on the part of the group as they see their crops being destroyed. There is great emotional disturbance consequent to this: fear, sorrow, anticipated grief and hardship. No doubt in some skeptical ones there is slight anger at the delay of God

in responding to supplications. Certainly there is rage and an unpleasant feeling of balked effort toward the insects.

6. The rather sudden appearance of the gulls with some perturbation at first that they might also be bent on destroying that which the crickets had not yet devoured. Thus, increased emotional toning is developed, that is, fear and anger toward the gulls that they might assist in the final consumption of the growing crops and thus complete the horror.
7. The unexpected, the amazing behavior of the gulls in devouring not the crops but the insects. This not in few cases but in great quantities ; their disgorging these, so legend has it, and their curious repetition of eating still more crickets. Here we have the surprise turn or climax of a socio-economic drama in real life. Here we see the operation of what Sumner called the aleatory or luck element in social crises.
8. The saving of the crops, then, led to giving thanks to God who is credited with sending the gulls, not to the gulls directly, since the religious cast of their minds prevented this more primitive response. There was also the verbal testimony in church gatherings about this " miraculous " solution. There is, in short, the religious thrill of deliverance from evil and a return to good. As Sumner puts it:

   The minds of men always dwell more on bad luck. They accept ordinary prosperity as a matter of course. Misfortunes arrest their attention and remain in their memory. Hence the ills of life are the mode of manifestation of the aleatory element which has most affected life policy. . . . Good or ill luck were attributed to superior powers, and were supposed to be due to their pleasure or displeasure at the conduct of men. . .

The aleatory element has always been the connecting link between the struggle for existence and religion.

9. Then came the raising of the gull to a place of religio-economic. significance and the placing of a taboo upon its destruction. It becomes a sacred object. Thus we see illustrated the fundamental nexus of religion and socio-economic life witnessed in all rudimentary societies.

10. There has come a whole local literature, history and folk-lore about the gulls among these people. Thus a legend has grown up about the crisis and its solution. Curious attributes of insight and intelligence have been given them, often quite contrary to fact.

11. Recently we have a final culmination in an object of veneration and communal attention, if not direct worship, which serves for the group as a rallying point in recall and contemplation of this miracle. That is, we have a monument to the gulls which is a kind of attenuated, amorphous totem pole, something which in more simple cultures might have played a very distinct role in the daily religious life of a people.

To mention the wider implications from this curious incident: In the first place one notes the importance of disaster or crisis in producing the taboo and the new folk-lore. No doubt a great many of our taboos and methods of social control arose in critical situations not unlike this one in general features. In the second instance, one must recognize the psychological factors in the situation, such as the arousal of intense emotions, the feelings of balked effort and the tendency to superstitious and magical thought processes when the common-sense means failed. Finally, the direction which the interpretation of this experience took was determined by the previous experience, by what the anthropologist calls the culture patterns, of the group. Thus, the development of real animal worship and the making of the gull into a true totem were probably prevented by the existence in the minds of these people of religious and social ideas of a higher and different order from those current in more primitive peoples.

3

CULTURE AND PRIMITIVE PEOPLE

CULTURE AND PRIMITIVE PEOPLES

A few decades ago it was common to regard primitive life as at the opposite pole from civilization, with barbarism, semi-civilization, and the ancient civilizations arranged in order to fill the interval. Each culture and each trait was fitted into the exhibit of the continuous rise of mankind to the beautiful summit on which contemporary civilized man stands. At the present time there is little tendency to depict all cultures as struggling toward this eminence or straggling by the wayside.

We now recognize that each culture may be going its own way and that these several ways do not necessarily converge upon the type of culture which now prevails in Europe and the Americas. We recognize also that the differences between races or groups are little more, and perhaps nothing more, than culture deep. Even civilized man and primitive that is, contemporary pre-literate man despite the contrasts in the forms of their respective cultures, are not very different in fundamental disposition.

No psychological gulf divides the savage from the civilized man, but owing to the absorption of each in his own culture and to the limita-tions which this imposes, the savage and the civilized man may der-stand one another as little as do those who have no common language. Yet they may have as much in common as have the Chinaman and the Andaman Islander when they are talking about the same thing in mutually unintelligible languages.

A culture is not only directive but delimiting as veil, that is, it makes it easy for its sharers to understand certain things but at the same time makes it difficult for them to understand certain other things, such, for example, as the significance of men's behavior in other culture settings. Hence the savage does not, even superfically, understand the civilized man. To do so he must comprehend the latter's culture, or at least a goodly portion of it. The converse is perhaps equally true: the civilized man who has little acquaintance with other cultures does not understand those who are outside of his culture, and his interpretations are usually nine-tenths prepossession and one-tenth erroneous observation or errant inference. It is significant, then, that those who have had most intimate contact with peoples of another culture are impressed with their fundamental similarity with ourselves, and are inclined to attribute the so-called differences to differences in the cultures.

"MAN IS ONE ; CIVILIZATIONS ARE MANY "

So far as my personal experience goes and so far as I feel competent to judge ethnographical data on the basis of this experience, the mental processes of man are the same everywhere, regardless of race and culture, and regardless of the apparent absurdity of beliefs and customs.

Some theorists assume a mental equipment of primitive man distinct from that of civilized man. I have never seen a person in primitive life to whom this theory would apply.

There are slavish believers in the teachings of the past and there are scoffers and unbelievers; there are clear thinkers and muddle-headed bunglers; there are strong characters and weaklings.

The behavior of everybody, no matter to what culture he may belong, is determined by the traditional material he handles, and man, the world over, handles the material transmitted to him according to the same methods. . . .

Anyone who has lived with primitive tribes, who has shared their joys and sorrows, their privations and their luxuries, who sees in them not solely subjects of study to be examined like a cell under the microscope, but feeling and thinking human beings, will agree that there is no such thing as a " primitive mind," a " magical " or " prelogical" way of thinking, but that each individual in " primitive " society is a man, a woman, a child of the same kind, of the same way of thinking, feeling and acting as man, woman or child in our own society."

Our advantage over primitive people is one of greater knowledge of the objective world, painfully gained by the labor of many generations, a knowledge which we apply rather badly and which we, or at least most of us, discard just as soon as a strong emotional urge impels us to do so, and for which we substitute forms quite analogous to those of primitive thought.

The much maligned introspective psychology proves to the unbiased observer that the causes that make primitive man think as he does are equally present in our minds. The particular behavior in each case is determined by the traditional knowledge at the disposal of the individual.

4 HISTORY OF SOCIAL CHANGE

Culture is not static, as might be assumed if the analysis of it were carried no further than in the preceding chapter; rather, a survey of cultures indicates that cultures change. Sometimes the change is slow, as in primitive societies; sometimes it is rapid, as in our own machine civilization. This dynamic quality is characteristic of culture. In contemporary society, in the Euro-American culture area, change is usually most marked in the material civilization. The automobile replaces the horse, and the airplane develops into a new mode of transportation with startling rapidity. In 1920 radio sets were rare — veritable scientific curiosities; in 1927 it was estimated that 7,500,000 homes were equipped with them. This is typical of many changes that have occurred within the past two generations. Such changes in the material civilization cannot but influence other phases of life. All parts of culture are intertwined into " a mode of life," and what affects one part must affect the whole. Habits, attitudes, philosophies of life — these, too, are changing. What have been termed folkways and *mores* are constantly undergoing adjustment, though not always with the rapidity of the change in the material sphere.

The purpose of this chapter is to examine into the

nature of culture change and to discover its underlying factors. Culture change and social change are terms used interchangeably, for social change *is* culture change. The fact of change is first introduced in the reading by Chase, who contrasts life today and three generations ago. After stressing the extent of the changes in the intervening years, Chase raises questions of evaluation that are worthy of serious contemplation. That change is not a phenomenon unique in our culture is suggested by Merz and the editorials from *The Nation*. A third introductory reading, again by Chase, indicates how culture changes modify daily life in minute detail, and almost unconsciously.

Culture changes at any time or place either as the result of invention or contact. If people devise something new (invent) the new trait is added to the already existing culture — which is technically called the culture base — where it either displaces older traits or exists beside or in amalgamation with the older traits. There is thus a tendency for culture to increase in complexity, and to accumulate.

Taking the world as a unit, all new traits, material or non-material, arise because of invention. A trait must be invented somewhere before it can be borrowed. The act of invention is closely related to the existing culture base, because the inventor utilizes the existing culture base and reworks traits that are a part of it, reshaping them into new combinations. While the inventor is a man of inherent ability, no inventor can go beyond his culture base if his invention is to be accepted. Invention as a factor in social change may be regarded as a cultural process. Professor William F. Ogburn, commenting on the social significance of invention, writes:

It may appear strange to the reader that an article on inventions and discoveries in 1927 which are reported largely in the mechanical and non-social field, should be included in a collection dealing with social changes. It is the belief of the writer, however, that such an inclusion is not only permissible but obligatory. For have not the inventions of the automobile, the steam engine, and correlated mechanical developments been responsible for profound social changes in such social institutions as the community and the family, as well as for far-reaching changes in social customs? It is also obvious that such mechanical changes very seriously affect the social welfare of human beings, for good or bad. Indeed, it may be argued with some success that the origins of most of the innumerable social changes occurring today lie in new inventions of a mechanical nature and in the scientific discoveries of natural science, though we cannot always foretell from the new inventions or discoveries what specific social changes will be precipitated. No apology on this score, therefore, seems necessary.

The reading by GilFillan develops this thesis, stresses the importance of the inventive process in social change, and especially emphasizes the *role* of culture itself in the inventive process.

That culture also changes as the result of contact is evident. One of two consequences may follow the contacts of peoples. There may be a general borrowing of traits from each other, or in one direction, with subsequent displacement of older traits or amalgamation with them. On the other hand, especially where the contact is accompanied by political subjugation and the use of force, the weaker culture may be totally disrupted, and disintegration follow, with nothing surviving except the traits that may be taken over and added to the culture base of the conquerors.

Not all inventions are accepted, nor do peoples borrow indiscriminately from those with whom they may have contacts that are peaceful. A selective factor operates, and in considering this the concept of *culture pattern* is all-important. In any culture area the traits and complexes, regarded in the abstract, have a definite arrangement. From the individual's point of view it can be said that certain phases of the culture assume greater importance than others:

The various culture areas illustrate mental patterns, and the mental pattern is as real as the cultural. There is in each culture area a type of mind reflecting and reflected in the various phases of the culture, responsible for it and responsive to it. The contours of the mental pattern are almost coterminous with the contours of the culture, and the content of one is reflected in that of the other.

Traits will be accepted, whether invented or borrowed, only as they can be adjusted to the culture pattern of the group. Unless they are adapted, or can be adapted, to the mode of life of the people they will be rejected.

It is this selective factor in the processes of invention and borrowing that Bartlett and Pitt-Rivers discuss. The latter also introduces significant material concerning the contacts between strong and weak culture groups. In the article by Mȩek the importance of contact in social change is demonstrated, and the way in which diverse cultural strains have fused as the result of borrowing — in what is known as the process of *syncretism* — is shown by Schermerhorn.

From what has been said it follows that the process of adapting new traits, whether inventions within the area, or traits brought in from outside, is always accompanied by some cultural disturbance, manifesting itself in human behavior. Sometimes the readjustment is simple and the disturbance trivial and momentary; sometimes it is fundamental, as the material by Pitt-Rivers amply shows. A series of specific illustrations bearing on these points is included in this chapter: Cavan shows how transplanted traits must be and are woven into existing backgrounds. and she draws her material from the field of missionary activity among primitive peoples. Cornelius looks upon the Christian missionary movement — an example of organized diffusion — from Oriental eyes, and sees how basic are the problems involved in transplanting a religion. An article by Gannett suggests that extensive borrowing may produce strange and often chaotic cultural inconsistencies— the hybrid being neither the new nor the old. The effect upon old institutions — culture patterns — of newly-introduced complexes is also described in Kelsey's article, which also recounts some of the " benefits " of Western civilization for which industrialism must be held responsible. (Yet the conditions sketched here are not so bad as those which prevailed in England a century ago.) Finally, the difficulties that are involved in engrafting new complexes upon old backgrounds are seen from Howe Wo De's discussion of the problem of mass education. A needed change would involve a complete disruption of important phases of the culture.

Acculturation is the process of adjusting to culture, and every cultural change introduces for individuals problems of acculturation. Fundamentally the acculturated person is one with well integrated habits. If an individual, acculturated in one area, moves into another, a problem of re-acculturation develops. Just as the culture in any area may change, so that part of culture which has become embodied, in the form of habits, in any individual or group of individuals, may and on occasions must undergo change. A radical change in habit is always accompanied by emotional disturbance; re-acculturation is accordingly often a tortuous process. Some of the problems involved, and the disruption of the emotional life with consequent loss of morale, are shown in the selections by Park and Kawai.

While invention and borrowing are the dynamic factors in the accumulation that is manifest in culture change, there are at the same time factors producing resistance to change. It may be said that all change is the resultant of two groups of forces: those inherent in invention and contact, and those producing cultural inertia. Many inventions, subsequently accepted, at the time of origin are resented,' and efforts are made to prevent their acceptance. The material by Smith illustrates this. Here the force of habit, the emotional set of the group, and the domination of traditional ways in the culture are merged to resist the new. This same domination of older cultural ways, the persistence of earlier cultural forms, is shown in the section by Wallis, who discusses the transplanting of a culture. Social isolation is likewise an important factor in inertia; without contacts the culture of a group changes slowly. Possibilities of borrowing are fewer, and " cross fertilization " of traits does not take place, as an article by Beynon

Survivals in any culture also foster conservatism or inertia. Survivals are traits which in their present form have lost their original utility — relics of a previous cultural state. Superstitions and superstitious practices are survivals in an age of science, as Sir James Frazer makes apparent. Not all survivals are non-material, however; but survivals in the material culture — cow-catchers on railroad engines or smokestacks on motor-driven liners — are less important in producing conservatism.

While old cultural forms may persist either with their original utility or as survivals, traits, complexes or even whole cultures may be engulfed and disappear. Many primitive cultures have gone, as the Pitt-Rivers reading referred to earlier in this chapter shows. In our own time and within our own area, phases of a culture may become dormant. The disappearance of Yiddish as described by Brody serves as an illustration. While complexes do thus become dormant and drop from use, it is clear that such losses are far offset by the accumulation process.

The preceding discussion has centered largely in the impact of cultures and the disturbances resulting from changes thus induced. Although the problem is not altogether different, in concluding this chapter it is necessary to stress the disequilibrium that results when within any one culture area one portion of the culture changes more rapidly than another. All parts of culture are interrelated and balanced ; therefore, a marked change in one part of the culture may produce grave maladjustment, and give rise to what Ogburn has termed *cultural lag*. Culture changes may thus produce social problems. In the abstract a social problem is a maladjustment between two or more complexes that are related; in terms of behavior, a social problem is the failure of an individual or a group of individuals to adjust properly to their cultural environment. Stein's analysis of the growth of the city illustrates the genesis of cultural lags, and the concept is further elaborated in the sections by Anderson and Mowrer. Here are social problems that are reflections of our changing culture. In a static, unchanging society there would be no social problems. Mowrer's contribution further shows how there may develop within a single city " culture areas " characterized by specific types of behavior.

THE FACT OF SOCIAL CHANGE : 1800—1930

In the year 1800 my great-great-grandfather was living with his family in a little farmhouse near the town of Newburyport, Massachu-setts. For the past five years I have been living with my family in New York City. As a test of progress, how much more abundant, more rewarding, is my life than his? He lived at the threshold of the industrial revolution — the first textile mill in America was built in 1802. I live on the crest of the greatest wave of applied technology that the world has ever seen.

Newburyport in 1800 was, with its outlying villages, largely a self-supporting community. The bulk of its food, shelter, and clothing was locally grown and fabricated. By and large — save for the town sot — every able-bodied person worked, and worked at making something useful. Despite the rigor of this economic necessity, the work produced bears the stamp not only of utility, but of a gracious and lasting beauty. I sometimes think that High Street in Newburyport is the loveliest architectural grouping in America — unless it be the village green of Old Lyme in Connecticut. An early Nantucket ordinance bears the phrase " mechanics and other artists," and as one looks upon the houses, the doorways, the glass, the pottery, the pewter, the hooked rugs, the masonry, the ironwork, the chairs, the tables, and the cabinets of that eighteenth-century period in New England, one cannot but believe that the town fathers of Nantucket spoke truly. While a few years later in the harbors of Newburyport, of Salem, and of Boston, the spars and halyards and cloud-like canvases were to rise, of what has been termed the most beautiful and vibrant thing ever fashioned by the hand of man — the clipper ship.

Here obviously was no product of labor driven and unwilling, but the expression of an age which gave to the shapes and colors of its materials vigor, imagination, and the sense of lives lived at the full. And it is dubious if these things could ever have come to birth at all without a wide participation in their creation by the bulk of the community. Here and there one finds an eighteenth-century architect, a ship-designer, a cabinet-maker of outstanding ability; but by and large the output flowed from hands unsung and unknown, too numerous to catalogue. It was the work not of an individual genius but of a general culture level. On this level my great-great-grandfather lived his life and from it drew his sense of values and his measure of happiness.

Let us run down the list of essentials and compare my life with his.

First, as to shelter. I live in a decaying Victorian apartment house up three flights of stairs in a dark and dirty stair well. In certain seasons, for as much as an hour in the afternoon, sunlight will make its way through one window in the kitchen and lie like some rare flower on the floor. Otherwise there is no sunshine, summer or winter. And very little light; and not too much fresh air. We open our windows, but we never, if we can avoid it, look out of them. The art of the jerry-builder has affected woodwork, plaster, and plumbing so that nothing is ever quite clean, or quite dry, or quite workable. My wife struggled with a New England housewife's conscience for two years and then, to save her sanity, strangled it. We have a bathroom it is true, we have electric lights and a gas stove. But is my housing today — particularly when children and their needs are considered — superior to that of my great-great-grandfather in his sunny, low-eaved, great-ovened farmhouse in the town of Newburyport? It is true that for the same monthly rental we might have secured a cleaner and more attractive apartment, but owing to the immutable laws of real-estate investment, it would have to shrink so in size as to be almost uninhabitable by virtue of congestion.

Take food. The food we eat is vastly more varied; it is probably richer and undoubtedly softer than the diet of my great-greatgrandfather. The softness has an unfortunate effect on our teeth, and one wonders if the whole-wheat grains, the fruits and berries fresh picked, the simple vegetables from the garden or the root cellar, did not constitute not only a more wholesome but a more toothsome and succulent diet. One grows weary of pale food in cans and bottles and packages —however meticulously sterilized, however flamboyantly advertised. Not only vitamins, but the very juices which act most powerfully on the salivary glands seem to be missing.

Take clothing. Again the variety today is as conspicuous as its lack of durability. As the jerry-builder has undermined housing, so the shoddy-maker has undermined textiles. Not that sound cloth cannot be made on the machine. I saw an overcoat recently which had been used continuously for ten winters — and showed no sign of wear. It was not, however, a product of the higher salesmanship, but was made of cloth tested for the United States Government and ordered for a military officer. Today the clothes my wife wears are, I suspect, more comfortable, more suited to the lines of the human body, than those of my great-great-grandmother — however deficient they may be in workmanship. But the clothes I wear — in town at least — are both flimsy and hideous compared with the knee breeches, the noble colors, the brave brass buttons of Newburyport a century ago. I doubt if in all the centuries since men wore clothes there has ever been a mode so ugly and so depressing as the somber cylinders which have encased us since the forties. Along with the smoke of the coal age came what might be termed the smoke-stack style for men. Just lately one notes the arrival of a special sports mode which admits color and line, but only an infinitesimal fraction of the population — at due and circumscribed seasons and places — can avail itself thereof. Undertakers' regimentals still constitute the last word for the bulk of the male citizenry.

Take health. There were no reliable vital statistics in Newburyport in 1800, but I doubt if the average duration of life was as long as it is today. I suspect that we spend more days per year incapacitated by sickness, but medical science pulls us through where the blood-letters of Newburyport only assisted the gentleman with the scythe. If you fell ill, your chances of dying were considerably greater in the old days, but you did not fall ill so frequently — you couldn't afford to. The net result is a lower death rate today, but for that advantage — if it be one in terms of abounding life — consider the price that we pay in the services of doctors, dentists, hospitals, X-rays, injections, inoculations, and the staggering costs of blasting water systems, sewage-disposal systems, garbage-collection systems, and public-sanitation systems generally into a congested city area utterly unadapted, through lack of community planning, to such arteries.

Take education. I send my two children to one of the best modern experimental schools. We have tolerated the bleak apartment chiefly to be near this school. Yet I gather that the bulk of the effort of thosecompetent women who operate this experiment in education is directed to the recreation in a hostile environment of those factors of craftsmanship, manual dexterity, awareness of nature, spontaneous play, which my great-great-grandfather's children received naturally, automatically, and costlessly in Newburyport. The world those children took to as a duck takes to water is now being searched for in the city's canyons with a large outlay for " equipment" and " material " and '? project study "; with a terminology altogether stupefying; and with no assurance as yet that, beleaguered by an environment in which child life is implacably ignored, the search will be successful. The public schools of course have never even thought of such a search, much less begun it. In respect to the three R's, however, instruction not only in the experimental schools but in the public schools as well is vastly more competent than it was a century ago.

Coming finally to intellectual life — the life of the spirit, not classed as a stern essential by economists, but nevertheless relevant to the parallel which we are trying to develop and supremely relevant to the question of living life to the full. New York City today possesses resources for stimulating the mind and the higher emotional centers that places it, at first blush, utterly beyond the Newburyport of 1800. (Incidentally, and in passing, it possesses resources for stimulating the lower emotional centers on perhaps an even more magnificent scale.) One can take one's pick of sixty theaters, scores of lectures, the opera, a dozen concerts, art galleries, museums, scientific gatherings, what not. The sum total on any winter's night is stupendous. And I, for one, in the face of such an intellectual feast, feel often like the historic centipede.

The centipede was happy quite
Until the frog in fun
Said, " Pray which leg comes after which? "
And wrought his mind to such a pitch
He fell exhausted in the ditch,
Considering how to run.

Or else, and more frequently, I try to keep up to some degree with the plays that are being talked about, and the concerts and lecturers and exhibitions that are being talked about, and the books that are being talked about. Which tends to leave me very little time in which to talk about things that are being talked about. My wife and I become two highly specialized automatons, gathering pollen with incredible dispatch from a hundred flowers, booming our way in subway and elevated train and taxicab, in and out of lobbies, up and down elevators, through revolving doors, but — and here's the rub — when the cultural debauch is ended, with so little opportunity to distill honey for our future joy and sustenance.

What is this world so full of care
There is no time to stand and stare?

And the most saddening thing of all to us is the hostility which New York offers to the making and holding of friendships. We have acquaintances without number and among them many whom we long to know better; we call scores by their first names, clap them on the shoulder, promise to call them on the telephone, assure them " we must get together for dinner." We do an immense amount of greeting and an immense amount of handshaking and an immense amount of promising and then, because we cannot maintain the pace, a quite colossal amount of what can only be called bare-faced lying. Almost never do we sit down in that atmosphere of peace and timelessness which is essential in the cultivation of friendship. And we find that good, unhurried discussion in this city is as rare as friendly intercourse. Perhaps the two are governed by the same relentless law. It was Goethe who said that a civilization should be measured by the excellence of its conversation. The keenest intellectual joy I know is good discussion. In it one participates, feels something of the excitement of thought-creation, is not bound speechless in a lecture seat to be thundered at from above. In all the four years we have lived in New York, I have not had a dozen good discussions. Rather I have gone to a hundred committee meetings with a watch in one hand and in the other a pencil which forever seems to be turning out budgets and lists of possible contributors.

God knows there is culture enough but it is a spectator's culture, a listener's culture, not a participant's culture. It is handed down at so - much a head including war tax. It is not the culture which the free citizens of Athens knew as they sauntered eager and expostulating through their academies, nor yet that cruder but still vital culture which drew every man who could walk to the New England town meeting a century and more ago.

Where does the balance lie? In terms of living as set off from mere existing, who lives the more abundantly, my great-great-grandfather or myself? Before you answer, note this point well. He was an average citizen of his community, economically speaking; while probably the joint income of my wife and myself is two to three times the average of my community. Compare him with the average New York family as you find it in the Bronx, on the East Side, in the wilderness of suburban Brooklyn. Where then does the balance lie?

I started to make an impartial survey, but perhaps I have tilted the scales. The tendency to become maudlin about the old days — particularly to a New Englander — is a powerful one. I have probably succumbed to it somewhat. Certainly Newburyport in 1800 was no Utopia. Discount, then, the parallel which has been recited by a wide margin of tolerance, and again, where does the balance lie? I confess Ido not know. But the significant thing is that there should be any question at all; that I should look back with eyes that are so often envious to a time when all the results of modern technology were non-existent. Finally I may be accused of unfairness in comparing life in a small town with life in a great city. Remember, however, my standard of reference is net welfare. I have included the life of the mind as well as that of the body. By and large, I believe that a properly planned city promises *more* in net welfare, and so I think the comparison is not an unreasonable one.

There is a machine today which can make nails one hundred and nine times faster than the blacksmith in Newburyport could fashion them; a machine which can make plows thirty-two times faster. Cotton sheeting can be made one hundred and three times faster than ever my great-great-grandmother could spin and weave it. And it is alleged by competent technicians that we have, in the energy released by the turbines and engines of America, the equivalent of the labor power of three billions of slaves, or nearly thirty servants for every man, woman, and child in the country. Why is it, in the face of such unparalleled technical improvement and engineering development, such a wealth of natural resources laid bare since 1800, that my standard of living in terms of vital values is so little better, if indeed it is better at all, than that of my great-great-grandfather; while the standard of living of the average family in New York City is almost certainly worse? How has this stupendous gain in technology, in control over the forces of nature, been drained away and wasted?

Machine production in terms of tonnage output is a meaningless, and if the output be guncotton, an actively destructive thing. Trade statistics, transportation load, steel output, even harvest yields are only wind to inflate the empty brains of small-town boosters until they are corre lated with the vital statistics of the day-by-day life of the wayfaring man. The wheels hum, the freight trains roar, the mines belch, the forests crash, the oil wells spout, the sand hogs curse, the cities reach their white pinnacles to the stars — and what do we who live here in New York today get out of it?

Not nearly as much as we ought. Not a tithe of what Fulton and Arkwright and Watt promised us. The world is full of stuff, but it is largely ugly, depressing, mean, or swanky stuff. It carries little nourishment for the human organism. This is no triumph of human intelligence. This is the defeat of human intelligence. This is a child smashing a microscope. This is waste — meaningless, destructive, gigantic.

SOCIAL CHANGE IN ISLAM

Summer of a year ago, I stood one morning in the Dolma Bagtche mosque and watched the Sultan climb a marble stairway to his prayers. Anold man, tired, last and feeblest spokesman of a line of despots living past their day: he seemed the perfect symbol of an order that was passing. Just about that time, it happened, a young girl in Smyrna, with an eye for Paris modes and manners, was married to Mustapha Kemal Pasha. Between the two — the old man on the marble steps and the young girl in Smyrna with a wardrobe of Parisian clothes — there is a gulf a good deal wider than the Bosphorus. But if the Sultan is one symbol; then young Mme. Kemal is another — quite as real.

For the new tendencies at work in Islam go well beyond political affairs. They touch the social side of life; especially the side of interest to the Moslem woman. Two years ago the government of Kemal prohibited polygamy in Turkey. Attempts are being made today to give it back its place of honor on the statute books. Five successive measures have been introduced to that effect in the National Assembly at

Angora. A leader of the Old Guard, Salib Hodja, asserts that in no other way can Turkey absorb an excess of a million women into the primitive economic system of the country. So far, however, restoration of the old order has been blocked. The weight of Kemal's own authority has been thrown against it.

To be sure, too much ought not be made of legislative battles on this score. For one thing, polygamy in Turkey is far less general than most Westerners suppose. It is primarily an economic matter; a budget for one wife is all that the average Turk finds he can afford. Moreover, age-old institutions of this sort — and there is no doubt that polygamy has a firm hold in the upper classes able to afford it—are scarcely to be circumvented by the passage of a single " law." A real change needs the slow growth of tradition to support it. What has been the mode from 700 down to 1921 cannot be rooted out in two short years.

Quite apart from this dispute, however, there is evidence of a more popular sort to show a changing attitude on the part of Moslems toward the rights and privileges of women. Mustapha Kemal does what no war lord in Turkey has ever thought of doing in the span of thirteen centuries: addresses a gathering of teachers in the town of Brusa, and declares that the regeneration of his country can be effected only if Turkish women " join equally with men in educating themselves and taking active part in the nation's business." Meantime you find the Moslem woman entering for the first time into public office. Recently the Ministry of Posts and Telegraphs began appointing women clerks, not so much for the fact that they were needed as because the government intended to make official recognition of a new regime. " Assistant Mail Clerk " in a rural bureau somewhere may not seem either an important or dramatic role; but in the Moslem East the innovation is little short of revolutionary.

With it goes a new activity of women in varied forms of social life. Turkey, for instance, has a counterpart of our Red Cross, called the Red Crescent. Women manage its affairs — conduct negotiations with foreign diplomats as well as Turkish traders. They take a hand in journalism; there are three publications edited today by Turkish women. They venture into social gatherings beyond the mark that centuries of tradition have posted as a deadline. On one hand comes the news that for the first time men and women are attending lectures side by side, in the meeting-rooms of the National Society for Education; on the other, news that at a *soirie,* recently, Turkish women took part in a public dance for the first time with members of the foreign colony.

Even the time-honored institution of the veil is causing a revolt. To be sure it is probable that on this point too the Western world has certain misconceptions. The veil is not entirely a matter of devotion to the Moslem code. One reason why it has been worn so faithfully and for so many years is doubtless because the Eastern woman is aware of the charm that lies in a touch of mystery.

Still, the veil has been made unwritten law. Its effect has been to checkmate women's progress toward a greater share of social freedom. And it is interesting to find, in many different parts of Islam, new proof that the Moslem woman is aware of that. Rebellion spreads through India, Egypt, Syria — even, it is rumored, to the streets of holy Mecca.

No doubt the young wife of Mustapha Kemal Pasha will accelerate rebellion's speed. Her first arrival in Angora saw her stepping from the train dressed for a ride in the parks of Paris: riding breeches, high boots, spurs and jaunty outing cap. " It was evident from the moment of her arrival," declared a foreign correspondent on the scene, " that she wished to emphasize one fact: in his campaign for the emancipation of the Turkish woman Mustapha Kemal Pasha can rely upon the full and active interest of his wife."

For centuries the Moslem woman has been a slave to custom and a slave to marriage: uneducated, overworked. What is happening to change her status is a shift in interest certain to be slow. But certainly the last few years have seen it gather headway.

Meantime the same undercurrents are at work elsewhere — the same modern sets of value gaining ground. In politics, for instance. Recently dispatches reported that the Assembly at Angora had " voted the establishment of a republic " and chosen Mustapha Kemal as President. Whether that report means a republic in the democratic sense or an old-time oligarchy, are questions for the future. But there is unquestionably a faction in the Assembly that favors the real thing. Its presence there is a new element in the affairs of Turkey as a state. And the spirit of change is manifest in different innovations which have found their way into the new Constitution. The Premier, for example, is to be responsible to his Assembly for government policy as a whole, instead of each minister being separately responsible, as in some of the Continental countries — or, as in the United States, responsibility being fixed by calendar.

Obviously experiments of this sort — attempts to give some meaning to the new theory of sovereignty reposing in the Turkish people — are experiments written in fresh ink on flimsy paper; it is a far cry from " sovereignty " to the Turkish peasant shoulder-deep in ignorance and next-door neighbor to starvation. Still, experiments like this have set a precedent for Islam. They are epoch-making in a world whose every change has been by inches, from Mohammed down to Kemal. Even the peasant and his ignorance have aroused new interest. The government at Angora votes funds for schools and teachers: a drop in the bucket compared with what is needed, but a hopeful sign on the part of an Assembly busy with a war. And meantime there is a new organization, called the " Bilki Yourdou," or " Home of Knowledge," arranging elementary courses for illiterate adults in more than one Turkish city. That Islam is increasingly alive to the importance of something more adaptable than its own old-fashioned sing-song methods of instruction, was indicated at Geneva. All through that stormy conference the one stationary point in Turkish policy was a guarantee that under no circumstances, regardless of what happened to the " capitulations," would the work of American schools and colleges be allowed to come to grief.

There are other straws to show which way the wind blows. Turkey tries out prohibition, talks about its " labor problems," much as we give precedence to those two issues in the West. With the first — prohibition — the Turks have come around from an experiment in bone-dry legislation to a plan for moderate restriction, under heavy fine; with the second — labor — two fair-sized employees' organizations are recruiting volunteers from a class of workmen who did not know that the world had such a thing as " unions " till a year ago.

Western modes and manners begin to make themselves at home. Even age-old Mecca changes. We think of it as a stone-walled village in the desert, a wholly medieval Arab town. But Lord Headley, the British Moslem peer who recently returned from a pilgrimage to the holy city, reports that it has telephones and telegraphs, automobiles and electric lights. Even morning papers.

You can trust the times. Another generation, and the Mecca pilgrim is almost sure to find a sports page and a rotogravure section.

The net results of what is happening to change the pace of life inIslam ought not to be overestimated. These are tendencies — not the earmarks of a finished process. Islam has a giant task ahead. We can say that much in all humility, without setting too high a value on our own upstart culture in the West. For, despite the empty speed that sometimes seems the most prominent product of the civilization we have built ourselves, the fact remains that West is far ahead of East in many things that matter: schools, health, comforts, respect and opportunity for women. The Moslem world needs frankly to face a reformation. As one critic, who ranks also as a partisan, has pointed out: " For all its modern political resiliency, the soul of Islam is still encased in its medieval husk."

A fair estimate, probably; and yet the scene is shifting. All these factors we have noted here. And another factor more substantial still: the development of a new unity in Islam.

For progress often hinges on communication. And so long as the Moslem world is a medley of twenty different cultures marching side by side through all the centuries from the sixth down to the twentieth, ideas must make headway slowly. The mere geography of Islam is a formidable fact: great areas of waterless waste-land cut by tarnished mountains.

All that, too, is changing — and will change more, with time. "The days of the magic carpet have come to pass," declared a cable dispatch from Jerusalem, perhaps a little too enthusiastically, within the last few weeks. But the basis for a prophecy is there. " Plans are in preparation, and this fall will see their perfection, for the establishment of a motor highway between Bagdad and Damascus." There are several projects under way. Mr. Norman D. Nairn, who heads one company with plans for a trans-desert route, points out that such a highway would have the important result of " facing Mesopotamia toward Eu-ronp instead of toward the East." Meantime of course a land route over sand is not the only possibility. Sir Samuel Hoare announces in the British House of Commons that a bi-weekly airship service across the Moslem world is being planned. The Government, he states, has accepted the project in principle, subject only to details of the contract being satisfactorily settled by the Treasury.

Again we deal with a project in its early stages; but already the desert highway has been pushed this far: a few months ago the Arab kings of Mesopotamia and the Jordan kept a tryst by airplane. . . . The magic carpet with a vengeance.

One more " new tendency in Islam," then, to be added to the list. The vast tract of desert which has defied everything save camel caravan for centuries, made travel an adventure, diverted Western theories four thousand miles around Arabia by sea, is threatened with the yoke of rapid transit. Upon the politics and the social life of Islam, there can be no doubt but that a re-made map would stamp its mark.

SOCIAL CHANGE IN JAPAN

Rickshas are going out in Japan — the motor age is coming in. Ten years ago in Japan 118,904 of these two-wheeled, man-power gigs were licensed; today fewer than 85,000. In Osaka, the greatest industrial city, the number has been almost cut in half. Horse-drawn carts just hold their own; but the motor vehicle is coming with a rush. Ten years ago there were 24 motor trucks in all Japan, today there are more than 6,000; the number of pleasure cars has leaped from 681 to 15,000. Intercity buses have already appeared on Japanese roads. Thus the Orient sweeps into the mechanical age. It was only fifty years ago that the first ricksha appeared, its jog-trot speed destined to drive out the slow walk of the sedan chairs, *kago* and *norimona;* now a running man is already too slow.

Japan is weirdly mixed of medieval and modern. A Buddhist priest who attempted to present a petition to the Crown Prince provided himself with a dagger to disembowel himself after so sacrilegious an act; and the chief of police who did not prevent his reaching the running-board of the royal automobile resigned in shame. On the other hand, Japan's Farmer-Labor Party has all the modern frills. The right-wing labor unions retired when the new party decided to admit Communists to membership. Oddly, however, it was the strong Peasants' Union which insisted on including the radicals. Now there will be two labor parties. Between them they represent only 150,000 organized workers, while the latest census figures report 3,128,000 men and 1,562,000 women in industry (the latter a significantly modern figure). In any case, registration under the new Manhood Suffrage Act is proceeding so slowly that Japan may have to fight another election in large part or. the old selective franchise. In diplomacy meanwhile, Japan is ahead of the West. She is actively in negotiation with China for revision of her thirty-year-old commercial treaty, and her methods reveal a thoroughly up-to-date understanding of the farcical art of international intercourse. The Japanese Minister and the Chinese Foreign Minister conferred for three days before China presented her note suggesting revision. Every comma, apparently, was discussed before the note was sent. And even then it was not published!

SOCIAL CHANGE IN DAILY LIFE

Our culture complex — as the anthropologists say — is changing, nay, has changed. While England and Germany still remain coal civilizations, the United States has become, with unheard-of rapidity, a gasoline civilization. The acid test of a culture complex is the nursery. In American nurseries the choo-choo gathers dust on the topmost shelf while the red racer holds the position of honor on the floor. Little Archie can tell you on the nail the make of every car that passes him. The grocer boy will call it a day any time to help you change a tire. Where is the urchin who has not mastered the calisthenics of the traffic cop?

Of a Sunday, in front of the Church of the. Immaculate Conception in Pittsburgh one may behold an impressive ceremony. One by one, all day long, motor cars draw up before the church door. A priest sprinkles each with holy water and pastes upon the car a seal which insures automobile, driver, and passengers the protection of St. Christopher, lately appointed the patron saint of motor cars.

Ten years ago the consumption of gasoline in the United States was 300 million barrels; today it is 800 million barrels. Ten years ago there were two million cars in the country; today there are over twenty million. It is gasoline which has girdled the country with 300,000 miles of magnificent highways; decreased distances between communities as no other form of transportation has ever done; and with the shrinkage, stamped identical habit patterns upon the citizens of Boston, New York, Atlanta, New Orleans, Kansas City, Nashville, Los Angeles, and Seattle. It is gasoline which now propels, in motor trucks, more gross tonnage of freight than the railroads move. The Florida boom would have been unthinkable without gasoline. In the last few years has appeared the strange phenomenon of gasoline gypsies — uncounted thousands of families on the march from one automobile camping ground to the next, the country over. It is gasoline which has made possible the mass production of week-ends — the synthetic gin is only a by-product — which has made the reclamation of abandoned farmhouses by city folks a major industry; which has quadrupled the radius between the skilled worker's home and his job; which has built golf courses and demoralized the working schedules — to say nothing of the pantaloons — of practically the entire business world above $7,500 a year; which has in the guise of the tractor revolutionized farming methods; which has created the road house, the night club, put the hot-dog industry on its feet; added stupendous efficiency to the art of banditry. No saxophone blows without a faint whiff of gasoline behind it; no silver screen can flicker without its parking lines outside. It is gasoline, not cosmetics, which has given the flapper her final polish, and made the boy friend what he is.

Which brings us to the folkways of courtship. No longer do we love by dim gaslight but by dimmed headlights — and gasoline. Cruise around the outskirts of any city or town on a summer night and note the parked and silent monsters up every lane, before every vista where moonlight sparkles on the water; tail lights glowing, and kisses warm above the steering wheel.

Dr. Watson holds, not without some show of reason, that what chiefly marks off man from the other animals are language habits. The influence of gasoline on the American language is profound. A whole new dialect of slang has been created, much of which in due time will force its way into accredited forms of speech. Coming down Tuckerman's Ravine on Mount Washington the other day, we overtook a girl in riding breeches, resting on a rock. " Pretty stiff drop," said we, obeying the courtesies of mountain trails. " Tough on the brake bands," said she with equal courtesy. "Step on it, kid"; "park your hat here"; " aw, put it in reverse "; " I've been goin' it on high for a month "; "a regular self-starter "; " flivvered out "; " throwing the Rolls Royce "; " a six-cylinder guy "; " you've got water in your mixture."

Gasoline will start the. next war; gasoline in airplanes carrying poison gas will win the next war — or end the career of *homo sapiens* — it is not quite clear which.

And now comes this aggregation of flat tires, the Federal Oil Conservation Board, and wants to conclude it all by giving us only six more years of gasoline production at the present rate in America. The threat is grotesque, inconceivable. A law must be rushed through Congress prohibiting it. From the roar of the gusher and the shrieks of the spectators to the last flying explosion in the muffler, gasoline runs —? the heart's blood of the nation. Six years —

and then a gasless America! The mind reels at the contemplation of it. What? No taxis, traffic cops, Dixie highways, one-way streets, better Buicks, Standard Oil companies, filling stations, schoolgirl complexion billboards, airplanes, football stadia (for how could they be filled?), five-ton trucks, Klaxon horns, 25,000 new graves a year, *Saturday Evening Post* advertising, Fifth Avenue buses road maps, dash-board arehitecture, lubricating oils, four-wheel brakes, Diesel engines, installment selling, " Punk-ville 4 miles, Goodrich Tires," Tumble Inns, submarines, Ye Olde Antique Shoppes, gunmen in Packards, back-seat driving, back-seat kisses?

America without gas is a pipe without tobacco, a hearth without a fire, a suit without trousers . . . Death rather!

5

Invention as a Source of Social Change

INVENTION AS A SOUECE OF SOCIAL CHANGE

" Blessings on the man who invented sleep," said the classic Sancho Panza; and the English balladist:

So I wish in heaven his soul may dwell

Who first found out the leather bottell.

Perhaps, indeed, he was thinking more of the inner spirit of the bottle, than of its outer integument. Anyway these oldtimers express a thought that is common today, the rule even, and which not even a single social scientist has shaken himself sufficiently free from, viz., that the great inventions were made by certain great men. We know the names reported for many of the inventors, chiefly Americans, which were taught us in unquestioning youth. Many heroes have been forgot, perhaps, but they were individuals, it is believed, and might be known. Here is Rear-Admiral Bradley A. Fiske, U.S.N., for example, a very distinguished inventor, author of " Invention, the Master-key to Progress " (1921), saying in it that to Daedalus are ascribed the saw, gimlet, plumb-line, ax, wedge, lever, masts and sails. " As no records show to us that the inventions just enumerated (except masts and sails) had been invented elsewhere, we may feel justified in inferring that they were invented in Greece by Dasdalus, or by some other man bearing a different name — or by some other men." Not one was. In some of his other passages, to be sure, the Admiral reflects a sounder sense of inventive history.

However, that all inventions were made by certain men, and the great inventions by great men, is the almost universal belief. But here a difficulty at once appears. The famous inventors are called great because such and such an invention is attributed to them. Yet we do not call a commander a great general for gaining one crucial battle, nor a poet great for one perfect poem. For a single achievement, however momentous to us, may have been an accident to its maker.

Now among all the inventors of whom popular history tells, only three, Archimedes, Ericsson and Edison, have been credited with more than one important invention. Others may have equaled them in genius, but not in mythologic luck. So leaving aside these three " great inven-tors," let us take up the "inventors" who did everything else and later the question of who were really great inventors.

Who invented the telegraph? Any American who has been through the eighth grade knows that it was Morse and Vail, in 1844. But there was an English commercial line seven years earlier, and the Germans credit the telegraph to Sommering, of Munich, in 1809, and in Switzerland there was an electric telegraph in 1774, and one was proposed in Scotland in 1753. The matter becomes rather confusing for the eighth grade. Who invented the friction match? There are so many claimants that we don't know who the devil invented it, and so have named it after Lucifer. Who devised the aneroid barometer? In Paris in 1848 two men, Vidi and Bourdon, each claimed it, with apparent sincerity, and different courts decided for each of them. But 152 years earlier the philosopher Leibniz had suggested such a barometer, describing it exactly. If we should really examine the roll of honors, from Archimedes, called the inventor of the pulley, to Marconi and the very de-serving but not indispensable Wright brothers, we should find that almost every claim is disputed, and rightly.

The chief reason for this confusion of parentage is that the process of making a great invention is totally different from the common understanding about it. A great invention is not a completed product, issuing at one time from the brain of one inventor. It is a multitudinous collection of little inventions, and is a growth of centuries. Had a single inventor to make the whole, he would need more hands than a monkey, more lives than a cat and more inventive genius than Pallas, Hermes and Loki combined. Let us illustrate this by the history of the steamship.

The first stage of an invention is the beginning of a desire for it. We find the utility of the steamship perceived by Homer, who sang of the marvelous, great, black ships of the Phaeacians, which without sail or oar or crew, sped swiftly to the remotest ends of earth, bringing back merchandise. Next, paddle-wheels descend from c. 527. In the 13th century Roger Bacon, from his experiments with gunpowder, glimpsed the internal combustion engine, and the means of fulfilling the Homeric desire. He wrote: " Art can construct instruments of navigation such that the largest vessels, governed by a single man, will traverse rivers and seas more rapidly than if they were filled with oarsmen." An apparent steamboat was patented in 1661, and one probably built in 1738, and we have a patent with description from 1729. But no success was to be expected from such craft, for their engines were wretched. Watt's double-acting expansive steam engine appeared in 1782, and the next year the Marquis de Jouffroy had built a great boat, not fast enough, at Lyons. Before the end of the century steamboats had been built by many inventors, especially Rumsey on the Potomac and Thames, Fitch on the Delaware, who realized good speed and long commercial use, and by Evans, and Miller, who in 1789 made 6 knots on the Forth & Clyde Canal. In 1802 on the same water Symington's *Charlotte Dundas* was a perfect success, save that she washed down the canal's banks. Presently John Stevens, of Hoboken, had speedy steam yachts on the Hudson, even with twin screws, tubular boilers and high pressure, excellent save for the damning workmanship in their motive plant.

Meanwhile Fulton, as we know from direct testimony, had been studying the plans of boats, and interviewing the designers, of every one of the important previous projects, in France, England and America. So had the other inventors been studying, the steamboat evolving out of joint experience; but none were so assiduous as Fulton. In all about thirty steamboats had been built, all in those three countries, generally in the order given. Fulton first built a 66-foot boat on the Seine at Paris, and obtained some speed but little attention and no success. So he returned to the great rivers of America, and in 1807 launched the *Clermont* in the Hudson, and steamed for Albany at 5 miles per hour.

There was apparently nothing new and valuable about this famous boat. Her engines were from Boulton & Watt, and in no way except in her proportions was she superior to or different from her predecessors. Why then was she more successful? Chiefly because Fulton had, with his forerunner Stevens, made one crucial discovery — the Hudson River — and got a patent on it! It was fitting that we celebrated together the anniversaries of Henry Hudson and Robert Fulton, for each owes his greatest fame to discovering the Hudson River, although each had been preceded by a navigator of its lower waters, and had pioneered more elsewhere. This river was the one best water in the world on which to run a steamboat. It was the *only* water which combined all the advantages of poor winds (for good winds would mean superior efficiency for sailing vessels), no tow-paths, trifling waves, a deep channel, no rapids, a long, straight route between centers of commerce, yet paralleled only by bad roads, with an intelligent population, no national boundary, and an abundant fuel supply. I am convinced that the lack of success of several *pre-Clermont* steamboats was mainly due to their faulty environment (and also inferior patent protection). The Hudson was the one proper water for such craft as they; and it is noteworthy that the Hudson has always continued to float the best river steamboats in the world. But a New York paper on the famous day said that Fulton's boat had been invented with a view to navigation of the windless Mississippi — Fitch's aim, which was attained before there was a successful boat in Europe.

I do not mean to disparage Fulton's genius: he was a most brilliant inventor of many other things; but he did not invent the steamboat in the *Clermont*. Nor did he later, fur, after rebulding, her at once and ably adapting steam to various types of vessels, and striving to monopolize steam navigation in New York waters, he died in 1815.

The reader has not been fatigued, we hope, by the voyage of the steamship from Homer to Fulton, for this is only the beginning of her trip, and we can best understand inventions in general by keeping full speed ahead. The *Clermont* was a crazy craft, unseaworthy, and slow as a geologic process. If steamboats had stopped evolving with her they would be as rare and unimportant to-day as dirigible balloons or intelligence at a horse-race. She is like the ape in our ancestral tree, which we left long ago, and glad we are to have left it. But this was her significance — once it was possible to make money out of steamboats, more and more craft were built, and each brought its little mite, or its valuable contribution, to the art of steam navigation. Each added its inventions, its improvements of detail, which enabled the steamboat to navigate more waters, to be swifter, safer, larger and more economical and effective in every way. So the number of launchings and the rate of progress steadily grew, with Robt. L. Stevens, son of Col. John, contributing particularly many inventions.

About the time of the *Clermont*, John Stevens had reverted to low pressure and paddle-wheels, and produced a small vessel of high speed. His and his son's *Phoenix*, launched in 1808, which first of steamers sailed the sea, when driven by Fulton's patent to the Delaware in 1809, was a better ship than the *Clermont*, with a simpler steeple engine and much better lines She presents excellent evidence of Fulton's nonnecessity, for it appears that she was designed chiefly previously and independently, beginning in 1805, and that there was likely as much give as take with Stevens. Thus we may not conjecture, but flatly state, that had Fulton never lived, the first fully successful steamboat would have been launched by the Stevenses at practically the same time and quite the same waters as the *Clermont*.

The ripening art spread slowly, and where most needed. The St Lawrence knew steam in 1809, and the wild but swift and windless Father of Waters in 1811. Not until the year after that was a steamboat successful on a river of Europe (the Clyde). By 1819 they smote the sea with the resounding paddle, for short coasting jumps. Not until 1838 could they cross the broad Atlantic, with its wind and waves, as efficiently as the sailing packets, and then only for cabin passengers. By 1893 half the world's marine tonnage was steam-propelled, but not yet has the steamship become so perfected as to be better on all voyages than the sailer (also constantly perfected).

A steamship like the *Leviathan* resembles the *Clermont* no more than she does the Flying Dutchman or a quinquereme. Perhaps every principle that was in the

Clermont is tucked somewhere aboard the modern marine monster, but her 60,000 tons are built up on inventions other and countless, millions of inventions. She has ears beneath the water, wherewith to hear the signals of the sea, when the fog lies over, and she has varied instruments as well to pierce the fog, hearing and making heard. The stockless anchor in her bow is an invention; and so are the machines that forged the mighty links of her chain cables. There are typewriters in her office, and elevators connect her decks. The anti-fouling paint on her keel is an invention, and the tools that made it. Cheap steel, such as makes possible her hull, has been called the greatest of modern inventions; and necessary for that steel were all the instruments, processes and sciences involved, from finding the iron's ore in Lorraine, to devising the giant's thumb and finger, that pinched her plates together with one-inch rivets, and left the surface smooth. Her turbine engines, propellers, endless electrification — these are new. So we might progress from her keel up to the wireless antenna, and find represented in her, or involved ashore, so many inventions that their very descriptions would load the ship. Scarce one of them is indispensable for a great liner, yet all help, and all the millions of them arenecessary to make her as she is. Few of these inventions were represented in the *Clermont*. The *Leviathan's* real inventors were half of all the fathers of devices or improvements who have lived since time began. She is a museum of modern civilization, riveted together and called a steamship. Fulton no more invented her than he did the moon. And just so is it with a printing plant, a telephone system or any other so-called great invention — each is the complicated product of a vast and age-old series of inventions in its own and all related fields, due to no one man, nor nation, nor century, nor millennium even. An " invention " is simply a certain grouping, defined by an English word, of all the achievements of men's minds since time began. So the " great inventions " were never made by any one — each is perpetually being made.

Why then is there that ridiculous common report, echoed even by inventors and engineers, that Fulton invented the steamship of today, or any steamboat? It is a matter of language, and of psychology. People want a definite origin for things. " Jubal: he was the father of all such as handle the harp and organ. And . . . Tubal-cain, an instructor of every artificer in brass and iron." The Greeks gave their thanks to Apollo for the invention of the lyre, if not to Hermes, to whom also they ascribed the alphabet, astronomy, numbers, weights and measures, the syrinx, music, gymnastics, tactics and olive culture. But let us consult a modern authority, the Century Book of Facts *(sic)*, "authentic, comprehensive, up-to-date," and published in 1902 in Springfield, Mass.. according to the title page, under the editorship of Henry W. Ruoff, M.A., D.C.L., and sometime professor. We read here, along with a typical chronology of modern inventions, that wine was brought from India by Bacchus, weights and measures invented by Phidon in the year 864 B.C., and that the reported inventions of Daedalus, which Admiral Fiske cited, were made in 1240 B.C. What admirable precision! And see Professor Ruoff's cosmopolitan responsiveness to the voice of authority: Wheat bread was invented by Ching-Noung, 1998 B.C; the flute and musical concord by Hyagnis, 1506 B.C; " it is, however, agreed that music was first reduced to rules by Jubal, 1800 B.C." Silk was invented by Se-ling, wife of the Emperor Hoangti, about 2637 B.C. (never mind if authentic Chinese history does begin two millenniums later), and the violin in 5000 B.C by Ravana, king of Ceylon. But as to weaving the compiler finds some difficulty, for the Egyptians ascribed the art to Isis, the Greeks to Pallas, and the Peruvians to the wife of Manco Capac.

A similar list, with mythology as bad, is to be found in *Le Machi-nisme Universel*, published in 1925 by Etienne Pacoret, " Ingenieur, Laureat de societes savantes et industrielles," author of seven books on engineering, perfectly competent in the engineering side of this his latest, but innocent of sociology, like the Admiral.

Now simply add an American myth that the steamboat was invented by Fulton. Primitive minds having their similarities, whether in Homeric Greece or Main Street, the recurrent question of whence something came, which it is known did not always exist, is answered by ascribing it to some definite and personal origin. " The telegraph? " Tom says, " why, some one must have invented it — it seems to me I've heard about Morse — yes, it must have been invented by Morse."

The popular idea, then, of an invention is a mythologic concept, a personal symbol to account for the origin of something. What determines the personage — why is Fulton called the inventor of the steamship instead of Roger Bacon or Symington or Thornycroft? That man is preferred as the titular inventor who belongs to our own national history if possible, or to a related country, and who was the first man to make the device a commercial success. Fulton was no more the first to improve the steamboat than he was the last, but he was the first to make money out of it. He is not deified just because he made money, but because his Clermont (with Stevens's Phoenix) was indeed a cardinal event in the evolution of the steamship. Previously, building steamboats had seemed a pretty sure way to lose money, so only a few fools built them. After the Clermont Fulton had money and reputation whereby to make further experiments, and other men were encouraged to build boats elsewhere, to make money. The more and bigger boats were built, the more inventions were made thereon, and the faster the steamship evolved. What Fulton achieved, through his lucky step of launching the right-sized boat on the right waters, was only to change the steamboat from say 95 per cent worth while (i.e., from a means of losing money) to 105 per cent worth while (i.e., a means of gaining money). There is a supremely important economic difference between a 5 per cent deficit and a 5 per cent profit — between the number of people who will enter a losing business, and a lucrative one. Yet the genius required to make that small increase of return was no greater than some later inventor's who raised the steamship's usefulness from 8,030 per cent to 8,040 per cent. So the attainment of commercial success is after all an event of much importance, from its causing a sudden increase in the rate of invention upon a device.

Well, so it is with the mythology of most other modern inventions — the Wright brothers for the airplane, Edison for the motion picture, Marconi for wireless, are selected out of the millions of their helpers, for having been the men who were conducting an invention, the gradual product of centuries, in that moment when it crossed the dividing line between commercial failure and commercial profit.

We have mentioned the tendency for the titular inventor to hail from the right country. The English believe that the steamboat was invented by Symington, the Scotch call Bell (1812) the father of the steamboat, the French swear by Jouffroy, and the Spaniards have a thoroughly mythical Blasco de Garay. Mythology does not relish heroes who wereforeigners. The American list of inventors allots most of the honors to Americans, and about all the rest to Englishmen (including Marconi who did his work in England). Perhaps these personal symbols, as parts of our national epic, our patriotic religion, are necessary or proper concepts for grammar school children. At any rate they are bound to be propagated while Americanization is the watchword, for they strengthen hero-worship and patriotism, combatting socialism. But at least let those who are old and sane enough to hear such truths about the great inventions as are known to any specialist, not repeat that parrot folly of assigning single personal symbols to the great inventions, on which millions of minds have toiled for centuries, and still toil. There is no more necessity for our believing in such an origin for the sewing-machine than there is for such an origin of man or coats or modern agriculture; and to continue doing so would be equally fatal to all understanding of inventions.

If we desire great inventors to look up to, for learning how to live and labor, let us reverence those discoverers in all lands who through a lifetime of successful inventing showed indomitable perseverance, egregious ingenuity, shining genius. Such heroes include (remembering their lives, not their mythologic attributes), Archimedes, Roger Bacon, the Marquis of Worcester, Watt, Fulton, the Brunels, the Stevenses and Stephensons, Ericsson, Edison, Siemens, Hiram Maxim, Elihu Thomson, Charles Scribner, Steinmetz, Emmet, Coolidge and others who have labored long, avidly and brilliantly to advance human life.

Technic progress owes a great debt to genius, although we know of no invention which seemed to necessitate genius for its solving. Even if there were such, the abundance of duplicate inventions shows that other geniuses would have sought and found the solution, if one failed.

So the common idea that the great inventions have been dependent upon the genius of a single man, so that if the great So-and-so had died of whooping-cough all history would have been different — must now appear erroneous, and it will appear absurd from a further examination into the social process and controls of invention.

THE SELECTIVE FACTOR IN SOCIAL CHANGE

We know that any social group that can be studied possesses an organization, institutions, forms of material culture and functions of a considerable degree of complexity, and that these are in many cases peculiar to itself and are the characteristics which we use when we wish to distinguish it from other groups. We know in many cases that the elements of these complex forms came to the group ready-made from some outside source. But within the group they have developed their own peculiar forms. Can we say anything definite about the social and psychological processes by which this development is effected?

Very broadly speaking two opposing views may be put forward. According to the first, the social group should be looked upon as a sort of receptive mechanism always tending to whittle down anything new which is brought to it into some form which existed before the new material appeared, but never directly responsible for the production of anything new on its own account. According to the other, processes of change affecting a social group, however they may be introduced, are continually being actively shaped into new forms and never merely assimilated to old ones. This may be regarded as a way of stating the old controversy between " contact " — which leans towards the first view — and " evolution " — which leans towards the second view — as the key to the explanation of the growth of social structure and functions.

Let us assume that the main stimulus to change in society comes from outside the group which changes. This may not be altogether true, but it is a good starting-point for discussion. Now obviously customs, or institutions, or traditions cannot be transferred from one group to another irrespective of the social conditions of the receptive group. No amount of " contact " will ever cause a group to take over anything for which there is no fairly obvious setting in its own culture. For much the same reasons, no custom, tradition, or institution ever is taken over by one group from another which does not very speedily suffer important change. The general direction of this change is to make the importation more like the existing culture. In a broad sense the more important and significant, socially speaking, is the importation the more marked are the changes it is likely to undergo. Thus it is safe to say that the similarities of culture which may justly be used as arguments for social contact are always of relatively detached, unimportant and odd details. I think it to be the case that genuine likeness of important elements of culture which have persisted for any length of time points to the view that such elements have grown up independently in the social settings in which they are found.

When a custom is taken over by one group from another, it is subject to change:

(a) by assimilation to existing cultural forms;

(b) by the dropping out of many elements peculiar to the group from which the custom comes;

(c) by retention, in many instances, of details peculiar to the communicating group, but apparently not very vitally connected with the central custom which is adopted.

Furthor, these three processes can all be treated as direct results of a social situation, and independently of a study of the attitudes of the individuals in the groups concerned. From all these changes there may result a custom which is not found anywhere else than in the receptive group in question, but they are not genuinely constructive changes, for they are achieved by a blend of assimilation, omissions, and retention of odd elements.

In every case, however, we have to try to treat the social group as possessing, not merely a social structure built up in its past but also a general trend of development. This trend of development need not be, so far as I can see, adequately represented in the mind of any individual member of the group, but it is nevertheless a genuine factor determining social change within the group. Thus when a custom comes in from outside it is changed, not only by assimilation, simplification and retention of relatively unimportant elements, but positively in the direction along which the group happens to be developing at the time at which the custom comes to it. Since this direction may perhaps not be fully realized — to say nothing about its being fully formulated — by any member of the group, the influence which gives a positive bias to changes in a certain direction which the group is moving towards, may fairly be called *social*. Moreover the general functions of this influence are certainly constructive, and can be seen particularly in the welding together of elements coming to a group from diverse sources and having historically very diverse significance.

This is what I wish to call social constructiveness. It is a characteristic reaction towards imported elements of culture adopted inevitably by all strong and vigorous groups. It means that imported elements suffer change both in the direction of existing culture and along the general line of development of the receptive group. It means that while it may well be the case that the stimulus to social change comes in the main from social contacts, important social forms may genuinely grow up within a group. Coupled with what I said in the earlier part of the paper I think it goes far to justify the view that striking similarities in important elements of culture are an argument rather for independent origin than for transmission of such elements from one group to another. Probably the main way in which " social constructiveness " is exercised is that all incoming cultural elements, whatever their origin, having to do with the same general sphere of life, will be dealt with by the activities which determine the trend of development of the receptive group in relation to the sphere of culture involved. Consequently they will be built together and worked up into forms the details of which come from varied sources. This is what makes it necessary to call the whole process constructive.

Clearly we want to know a lot more about the precise mechanism of the process which I have characterized in general terms only. As I have said, I believe that the main underlying basis of this type of change is truly social and cannot be expressed in terms of individual psychology. But no doubt individuals of a dominantly constructive habit of mind do play a large part in the mechanism by which this social tendency finds concrete expression.

6

CULTURAL CONTACT

SOCIAL CHANGE AND CULTURE CONTACT

1. The Native Problem

Under the vague and somewhat ambiguous title "Native Problem" are grouped all the problems and difficulties that have arisen in every part of the world where European Christendom has taken over the control of the destinies of backward and dark-skinned races. The term itself, and the constant references that are made to it in connection with the almost ubiquitously existing state of unrest among subject races under European tutelage, implies that the " problem " is unsolved. Western civilization has assumed control of subject races but has as yet failed to stabilize the relation between subject and ruling race and between two incompatible cultures. But the problem, so long as it remains a problem, has two sides to it. There is the problem of realizing the white man's interests in a black man's country — that is the former's aspect of the problem; and there is the black man's problem — the problem of maintaining his own existence, identity and welfare. Neither side should be considered without the other, for they are both part of the same problem. In practice this is far less often remembered than might be supposed.

The problem exists throughout the world. We are asked to consider the Native Problem in South Africa, every day growing more insistent. In America the problem of the Negro becomes ever more acute; only owing to his fast dwindling numbers the Red Indian and the Eskimo are less anxiously regarded. In India and Egypt we face tumults and agitations for self-government; in the surging aspirations of Pan-Islamism we faintly recognize a challenge to the white race and a rejection of its culture. In China the challenge is distinct and menacing. Even in New Guinea, where the problem is newest but not less urgent and the natives still inarticulate, we are constantly reminded of the growing difficulty of securing native labor for the plantations, and of their growing insubordination or disinclination either to work themselves or to breed workers for the white man.

2. The Relation of Race to " Culture"

The relation of culture to race has long been a problem that has exercised the minds of anthropologists. Like most debated problems the answers all depend upon the way the question is framed and the terminology used in framing it.

The problem is but an aspect of the problem of all organic life: it is the problem of adaptation; and adaptation, we have been perhaps rather late in recognizing that fact, involves mental and cultural no less than physical factors.

If, then, I may restate the problem in terms which I think most clearly define it, it may be summed up by saying that the culture level of a people at a particular time is conditioned by three factors: by their heritage of *culture-forms* (traditions, art-forms, beliefs, customs and social organization), together with *culture-accessories* (implements, weapons and mechanical discoveries), and by their *culture-potential* (a term here applied to innate constructive ability;

power of expression; the capacity to develop, under suitable conditions, artistic, scientific or technical skill; and temperamental disposition). Culture-forms and culture-accessories are not simply bequeathed to a people and in turn handed on by them intact, but are evolved and modified by successive generations; while at every stage culture is conditioned by the capacity of people to give expression to it.

We have to face the problem of racial capacity to become adapted to changed environmental conditions. An examination of population tendencies in the Pacific regions and in America appears to show that people are far less adaptable to great and sudden changes in culture-form than is generally supposed. The more specialized a people become through segregation and the agency of selection, the more closely adapted are they to the culture-forms they have evolved. Any drastic change in mode of living and in culture-form imposed upon them from outside and not evolved or modified by themselves leaves them, for this reason, ill-adapted to the innovation. It is a psycho-physical problem, the physical consequences of which are illustrated in the phenomenon of the gradual extinction of unadapted peoples. This conclusion is supported by an analysis of the demography of peoples all over the Pacific and in America, where a biological substitution of population is taking place. Apart from a systematic analysis, however, the facts are apt to be obscured by the gradual infiltration of foreign blood into a declining population, and the frequent inability to discriminate between the unadaptable and unmixed stock that is declining and the new mis-! cegenated stock which is capable of surviving under the changed conditions.

Briefly summarized the effects of the contact of two dissimilar, but interacting culture-trends, can be grouped under the following classes:

1. Immigrant and more powerful culture-bearers may so

revolutionize the environmental conditions of the native and culturally weaker people that, incapable of readaptation, they become eliminated and die out — examples, Tasmanians, and some Australian, Polynesian and Melanesian tribes; or

2. The elimination of the people of a weaker culture may be disguised by a blood-dilution which gradually changes the ethnos or ethnic continuity of the population, substituting miscegenated stocks, more adaptable to the changed cultural conditions, which gradually take the place of a former population — instance, the Maoris of New Zealand.
3. A people forcibly removed from their own culture environment and transplanted into another, where they are preserved and bred, may become adapted to new cultural conditions, with a minimum of change in ethnic continuity. Example, the Negro population of the United States during the period of slavery.
4. Gradual culture assimilation and amalgamation of aboriginal people by immigrant people. Example, the Polynesian assimilation of Melanesian or Australoid peoples.
5. The relative segregation of small cultural pockets maintaining themselves within the sphere of influence of a stronger culture. We might perhaps cite some of the Lolo communities near the Tibeto-Burmese border in Southern China.
6. Strong immigrant culture-bearers may meet with strong and persistent opposition on the part of natives who may resist cultural contamination with great determination. I think particularly of the Bali-nese peaceful, but stubborn, rejection of all European cultural influences, or of the traditional Chinese intolerance of European proselytism, provoking,

however, a more emphatic demonstration.

7. Immigrant culture-bearers may succeed in extinguishing an aboriginal culture, but yet fail either to extinguish or assimilate its hearers, who appear to survive the condition of cultural disequilibrium. May we here not cite some African examples, among, for instance, Basuto or Bantu tribes; and finally —
8. We may be reminded that the indigenous elements may eventually absorb the immigrants and assimilate them with or without taking over much of the culture of the latter. Here, for instance, we may think of the assimilative tendencies of the Chinese, who appear to have assimilated even the Chinese Jews who in physical features, language. dress, habit and customs, in fact in everything except their religion, appear Chinese.

3. Overpopulation and Depopulation

In every instance where one culture strongly influences another, a condition of culture disequilibrium is engendered, followed by the extinction or modification of the weaker culture and a variable degree of readaptation accompanied by a greater or lesser change in ethnos.

When two races meet there are three ways by which one may extinguish another. Directly, by violence; by gradual substitution through differential birth and survival rates; and, thirdly, when they mix freely by selective elimination of less adaptable characters. We often confuse the decline of a race and the decline of a population. The infiltration of alien stock may check the decline of population, while, at the same time, the racial elements continue to decline.

But the cultural clash resulting from one racial group dominatinganother does not always initiate a state of depopulation — it may promote the opposite. India provides an instance. Here the opposite of depopulation is occurring.

Whether it amounts to overpopulation or not does not much matter for our present purpose. It is interesting, however, to note that Professor Carr-Saunders not only believes that overpopulation occurs in many parts of India, but assigns as responsible for it very similar causes to those which are also responsible in different circumstances for the opposite tendency — for the depopulation of subject races.

It appears, then, that under certain circumstances when a people fall under the domination of an alien race, which seeks to impose upon it incompatible culture-forms, overpopulation, or at any rate an increase of population, is likely to occur, partly as the result of the breakdown of native customs, which formerly regulated numbers, and partly by inducing a feeling of general discontent or of apathy or by fostering a condition of social disorganization resulting from interference with, or modification of, native cultural elements. But, as we shall have further reasons for believing, it is also in the break-down of native customs and the suppression of the native culture by the attempted imposition of incompatible culture-forms that we find the principal causes of the depopulation and gradual extinction of many of the races subjected to European government. At first sight it may not appear consistent to attribute exactly opposite results, both depopulation and overpopulation, to the same group of primary causes.

We may, however, provisionally distinguish the group of circumstances in which the " culture-clash " fosters increasing population or overpopulation and the group in which it tends to bring about depopulation or a decline of population. Perhaps the most conspicuous difference between the culture-clash in India and Indonesia with their teeming populations and the culture-clash in the depopulated islands of Oceania, or as applied to the aborigines of Australia and Tasmania, lies in the capacity shown by the Hindu and Moslem cultures of the former group to resist the European proselytism which they despise, and to preserve almost intact their traditional cultural values, however drastically their economic and political evolution may have suffered modification, whilst the barbarian cultures of Oceania and Australasia, conscious of their cultural and intellectual inferiority, have been powerless to preserve the essential elements of their cultures against proselytism.

In India native unrest became serious only in recent years. There is no question, here, of the eradication of native culture; native culture is highly evolved, complex, and resistant, and the tiny population of white colonists is quite incapable of imposing its culture upon the intellectual classes and leaders of thought, either Hindu or Moslem, who are the guardians of the culture-forms of the different races in the country; neither is it able by its influence so to modify the social organization or so to revolutionize the living conditions of the people that they are in danger of losing all interest in life and dying out, like the less highly cultured and more defenceless Polynesians and Melanesians of the Pacific. Nevertheless, the influence of European rule upon native life is considerable, but in place of tending to exterminate it has had the result of greatly enhancing the pressure of population, and at the same time fostering a growing spirit of discontent. Sir George Birdwood points out that sheer pressure of population aggravated by the reduction, under our benevolent rule, of the virulence of plague and of the frequency of famines, and of such checks to overpopulation as abortion and infanticide, has contributed to the underlying physiological causes of manifold discontents. More important, however, and less subject to dispute, are the psychological factors which now produce the growing discontent of Indian peoples with the condition of European rule.

The attempts at Europeanization, to the extent to which they have met a successful resistance, have, as an inevitable consequence, produced, and been the measure of, the " unrest" that distinguishes the native problem in those countries; whilst the impotence of the more lowly and barbarian cultures to make an effective resistance has left the natives ill-equipped, and without the will, to survive the destruction of all the values that gave meaning and zest to their lives. The same forces that have in the first instance only succeeded in modifying and hampering the normal expression of native culture-forms at the cost of social disintegration, have in the other led to the extirpation of native-culture forms, with the consequence that the natives have failed altogether to adapt themselves. The evidence for the correctness of this explanation must be left over until detailed illustrations are given. Another factor that has aided the subject races of higher culture in their resistance to all attempts at Europeanization has been their overwhelming numbers in proportion to their European invaders, who have failed to colonize and increase rapidly in a climate to which they are not innately adapted.

4. Causes of Depopulation

This explanation, it is true, oes not apply to every country where the clash of culture occurs between ruling and subjugated races. For instance, the Bantu is a lowly and banbarian culture, ill-equipped to resist European colonization, yet the Bantu races are not dying oat. Again, the Negro is far from dying out in North America, although the North American Indian is left behind in the race by both black man and white.

According to the view that I am now presenting, these contrasts in the effects of the culture-clash all depend upon the adjustment of widely differing external and internal factors. Such factors are:

1. Variations in the relative power of the dominant culture in influencing the normal living conditions to which

the natives are adapted.This factor varies according to the extent of effective interference and control exercised.

2. Variations in innate amenability or adaptability of the subjugated races. This factor is equally as variable as psychological types. The grounds for supposing that distinct fundamental differences in psychological type exist will need separate discussion.

3. Modification and transformation of innate qualities of subject races by the infiltration of alien blood. The influence of race-mixture must be left over for a separate investigation.

Human fecundity, or the capacity for natural increase, is normally so much greater than the greatest possible fertility compatible with the available means of subsistence that in all populations — except those that are dying out —any increase in the factors of elimination tends to be compensated by an increased fertility, which is still far below the rate that fecundity makes possible.

It is too often assumed that the decline and disappearance of a population is wholly due to the operation of new or of old factors of elimination. When a decline is observed, any new factors, or any factors that have been and are still operating as checks to population, are immediately cited as sufficient cause to account for the decline, without pausing to consider why fertility — always so far behind fecundity — can no longer keep level with the factors of elimination. When, as sometimes happens, a population declines, and at the same time many of the old factors of elimination are removed, as when the Maori population was observed to be declining during the last three decades of the nineteenth century, although warfare had ceased to be a factor of elimination and food was more abundant than ever before, the most contradictory and diverse causes are often arbitrarily cited by baffled investigators to account for a phenomenon they cannot explain.

Although it is well known that a high mortality rate is the normal accompaniment of a high birth rate, and a low death rate the normal accompaniment of a low birth rate, exclusive importance is often attached to the factors and the rate of elimination while ignoring the relation of one to the other, as well as neglecting to discover the underlying root causes determining the adaptability or inadaptability of a population-to changes and influences, both physical and psychological, in their environment; and forgetting that the factors of elimination, whether many or few, are the agents whereby the fundamental tendency in adaptation is able to express itself. Where there is adaptation the elimination rate meets requirements by maintaining the population at its " optimum density "; where there is failure in adaptation elimination may exceed, and a progressive decline will be witnessed.

The remedies proposed at different times to alleviate or cure the decrease or degeneracy of the people may similarly be classified according to whichever view is taken of the causes of decrease. If the effective causes are primarily due to conscious or unconscious influence or interference on the part of Europeans, the remedies must logically lie in removing those influences or in counteracting them; if, however, they are Inherent in the native life and system, a remedy may then be found in bringing a still greater influence and a more effective interference to bear on the natives.

A survey of the important Reports and of the recognized literature on the subject shows a curiously persistent tendency to lay the weight of responsibility for the decline on elements inherent in the native culture. Thus Sir Hubert Murray, Lieutenant-Governor of Papua, in his ' Review of the Australian Administration in Papua from 1907 to 1920 " after expressing the opinion that the original tendency to diminution had spent its force so far as the territory under his administration as a whole was concerned, speaks of " other tribes," mentioning as examples the people between the Fly and Pahoturi, " who, apparently, must disappear before long, and when one considers their habits, the only cause of surprise is that they should ever have come into existence at all". Definite mention is made only of child-marriages, and "the probability of unnatural offences, and other filthy customs," He then continues: " People of this kind must die out in any case, whether white men come or not, and their existence shows how the problem is com-riiieated by the absolute lack of evidence whether the population was increasing or decreasing before we came to Papua. It is difficult to imagine that people with such habits as those mentioned should ever increase." Were it not for the prevalence of this sentimental and unscientific view, which is likely to remain attractive if for no other reason than because it seeks to exculpate European civilization from a charge of exerting a lethal influence, it might be unnecessary to labor the point that there is no necessity for people who practice child-marriages, even coupled with " the probability of unnatural offences and other filthy customs," to die out in any case; and whether it be difficult or not to " imagine that people with such habits should ever increase," it remains a fact that child-marriage, together with innumerable habits strongly distasteful to European sentiments, have prevailed among people over a very wide region, including India, who have yet shown remarkable powers of increasing.

THE FUSION OF TRAITS THROUGH CONTACT

It used to be said that the Hebrews owed their uniqueness to the fact that God had separated them from the rest of the world and had given to them what he denied to others, as if one could " isolate a people and treat it as a unique phenomenon in history, as a flower that bloomed solitary in some divine or magic garden, without striking roots in the common earth, without breathing the common air, without expanding in the common sunshine." If history has taught us anything it has taught us this: that nations never lived in watertight compartments, in splendid isolation one from the other; and least of all did the Hebrew nation, situated as they were on the great highroad between east and west. With alien caravans and armies constantly passing through their very midst, they could not have remained aloof from the world even though they had so desired. Instead of developing their unique characteristics because of isolation from the world, it was actually because of contact with it. Nations are like individuals. That nation develops most that borrows most. The most original of peoples appropriates most, drinking deeply from the common heritage of mankind. It was just because the Hebrew people lived in such intimate contact with the world and borrowed so largely from others, thus adding the attainments of others to their own, that they so far outdistanced their contemporaries in real cultural development.

An outstanding evidence of the penetration of alien cultures into that of the Hebrews is the very language in which the Old Testament is written. The Hebrews, by their own testimony, were of composite origin. The original stock was evidently Aramean, as Deuteronomy 26:5 asserts. In their early home in Mesopotamia and in their migration into Palestine they seem to have amalgamated to some extent with various " Hittite " groups, and in Palestine they gradually absorbed the native Canaanite-Amorite population. Hence Ezekiel (16:3, 45) could say of Jerusalem: " Your origin and nativity are of the land of Canaan; your father was an Amorite, and your mother a Hittite." The early Canaanite settlers in Palestine had been conquered by the Amorites, who, during a considerable sojourn in Babylonia, had absorbed much of Babylonian culture. This is evidenced by the presence of many Babylonian loan-words in the Amarna letters, which are glossed by Canaanite words for their better understanding. The Amorites in turn were conquered by the Egyptians, who held the country under their sway for many centuries and left an indelible impression upon the land and its people, as recent excavations are making all the more evident. Moreover, a part of the Hebrew people spent some little time in Egypt, and must unquestionably have brought Egyptian influence and blood back with them, which in course of time they communicated in some measure at least to their compatriots in Palestine. Hence the Hebrews from the very beginning were open to all sorts of influences, and in their ethnic composition were a conglomerate of many different stocks, all of which is very apparent in their language. Hebrew is full of loan-words from other languages, some of which came in at the very beginning of Hebrew history, and others in the course of the centuries of foreign contacts that followed. Hebrew, for example, has two words for " I," one 'anoki, identical with the Accadian (Assyro-Babylonian) anakn and the Egyptian 'nk, the other 'dni, identical with the Arabic 'and Similarly it has two words for " God," 'el and 'elohim, the first reflecting the Accadian ilu, and the second the Arabic 'ildh. The word for " palace," hekal, is a loan-word from Sumerian by way of Accadian. In Accadian it is ekallu, and in Sumerian, e-gal, literally, " great house." One of the words for " river," ye'or, is an Egyptian loan-word, while another is nahar, identical with the Accadian ndru and the Arabic nahru. One of the verbs " to see," ra'ah, corresponds to the Arabic ra'a while another, hdzah, is the Aramaic hdzdh. In Daniel alone there are some fifteen Persian loan-words and at least three that are Greek. Even the common word sus, " horse," was derived from the Indo-Iranian a'swas. These are only a few out of dozens of examples that might be given to illustrate the composite character of the Hebrew language, and this could be further demonstrated by the evidence of its grammar and syntax. In fact, it is only with a knowledge of the languages of all the peoples with whom the Hebrews came into contact that one can fully understand their language and accurately translate it. Many a difficult word or construction finds easy explanation when referred to the language to which it belongs and from which it came into Hebrew. . . .

The Old Testament contains a considerable account of the Hebrew sojourn in Egypt. Here, of course, the story demands an Egyptian coloring; but the remarkable thing is that the local color applies, not to Egypt of the time of the story, but to Egypt of the ninth century, when, according to modern scholarship, the story or stories were written. The personal and geographical terms belong for the most part to the twenty-first ?.and twenty-second dynasties, indicating that the author got as much from his own knowledge of Egypt as from tradition. The story of Joseph and Potiphar's wife is so identical with the popular Egyptian " Tale of Two Brothers " that the two can scarcely be of independent origin. Stories of this sort in ancient times, as in modern, traveled over the world, and were doubtless as well known to the Hebrews as to others. The Babylonian story of Ahikar, known to us in so many versions, Aramaic, Syriac, Arabic, Armenian, Ethiopic, Old Turkish, Greek, and Slavonic, similarly finds its reflection in the Old Testament. In the Aramaic version of Ahikar, for example, Col. VI, 81 f., " Withhold not your son from the rod, if you cannot keep (him from wickedness). If I beat you, my son, you will not die, and if I leave you to your own devices (you will not live)," we have manifestly the prototype of Prov. 23:13 f., " Withhold not correction from the child. If you beat him with the rod. he will not die; if you beat him with the rod, you will save his soul from Sheol."

Of all the literature in the Old Testament, that which would seem to be most purely Hebrew and unadulterated by foreign influence is prophecy; but even here scholars are now quite generally agreed that there is dependence upon

Egypt in both content of thought and literary technique. Eduard Meyer long ago posited a considerable dependence of the Hebrew prophets upon Egyptian seers; and recent writers in the field, although more conservative in their conclusions, are quite as fully persuaded of the fact. One outstanding characteristic of Egyptian prophecy, as both McCown and Gressmann have indicated, is the peculiar combination of threat and promise, and this finds its reflection in the Hebrew prophets. Many scholars, like Kemper Fullerton, would make all the messages of hope in the early prophets spurious; but Egyptian parallels would lead us to believe that unless there are strong evidences to the contrary, there is just as good reason for accepting the genuineness of the promises as of the threats. A good illustration is Deuteronomy 32, where, in a poem undeniably a unit, there is a sudden transition at verse 26 from the severest denunciation of Israel to the glorious promise of the following verses. The poem may be late, and the phenomenon is confessedly more common in later prophecy and apocalyptic, but that does not make it any the less Egyptian in its origin. Another likeness in literary technique is the pseudonymity of many of the Hebrew prophecies and apocalypses. This practice was a very early one with the Egyptians. It gave a writing more weight to put it in the mouth of an ancient worthy, and both the Egyptians and Hebrews did this to a degree unparalleled by any of their neighbors. More remarkable still is the fact that it is in the prophetic writings of the Egyptians and Hebrews alone of the ancient Semitic world that there is a passion for the regeneration of the social order. This is the reason for the threats and promises of the prophets; by their threats and denunciation they stroye to bring about a new order, which in both countries came eventually to be conceived of in terms of the Messianic era. The fact that the ideals of the Hebrew prophets surpass those of the Egyptian would suggest that they took up the ideas of their predecessors and carried them farther; and this too is the testimony of history.

The book of Daniel has affinities with both Egyptian and Babylonian literature, and the presence of Persian and Greek loan-words in it suggests other connections as well. On the Egyptian side the book is strikingly like the Demotic Oracle-Commentary, compiled at the end of the third century, B.C. The authors of both have the same point of view; they present the events of the past in the garb of a vision of the future, in many instances recording the same events; while their real predictions come only at the end, and are intended to encourage a discouraged people. On the Babylonian side many of the symbols and pictures are clearly of Babylonian origin. This is particularly true of chapter 7, where the " Ancient of Days " is represented as sitting on a throne of judgment, surrounded by myriads of attendants, and about to open the books of fate. Once every year in Babylon the gods assembled in " the chamber of destinies " and, under the presidency of Marduk, fixed the destinies of mankind for the coming year and had them recorded on " the tablets of fate." The reference to the book of life or fate is fairly frequent in the Old Testament (cf., e.g., Pss. 69:28; 87:6; 139:16; 169:9), and the popular Jewish tradition makes God function at the beginning of the new year exactly as Marduk did. . . .

It has long been noted that the Hebrew law codes offer many parallels to Babylonian law. At least hah" of the laws in the Code of the Covenant (Exod. 20:23-23:33) have their counterpart in the Hammurabi Code. and in many cases the likeness is so close that the one must surely depend on the other. Many of the Babylonian laws, we know now, had their origin in Sumerian law, so there can be no question as to the side from which the borrowing came. The Hebrews, according to their own traditions, once lived in Babylonia, and with their settlement in Palestine there came Babylonian influence through the medium of the Canaanite-Amorites. As Waterman has well shown, the Hammurabi Code in an adapted form was known in Canaan long before the arrival of the Hebrews. It is not often that there is verbal agreement between a Hebrew and a Babylonian law, but the variations are easily accounted for by the differing conditions in Palestine, by adaptation and elaboration. An example of close verbal agreement is Exod. 21:16, " Whoever kidnaps a man and sells him, or if he is found in his possession, must be put to death," and Hammurabi Code, 14, " If a man kidnaps another man's son who is a minor, he must be put to death." More significant, however, than verbal agreement is the frequent identity of technical terms. In both, for example, appears the expression " bring before God," by which it is meant that the case is to be brought before God for his decision, probably by means of the sacred lot or by ordeal. Th3e Hammurabi Code recognizes three classes of people: citizen, or awilum, literally man; conquered population or serf, muskenum; and slave, wardum; and so does the Hebrew law, with its 'ish, literally man; ger or toshdb, serf; and slave. It would seem to be something more than mere accident that there should be similarity like this.

That the Babylonian culture was one stream that helped to make up Hebrew culture is evident from the very first pages of the Old Testament. The early stories of Genesis are all set in Babylonia, and this would be most unlikely if the stories were native to the Hebrews. The Hebrew story of creation does not suggest many points of contact with the Babylonian, but that of the flood assuredly does. According to the Babylonian story, the gods in assembly decide on the destruction of mankind by a flood; Ea, however, reveals the purpose of the gods to Ut-napishtim and advises him to build an ark, which he proceeds todo, following the plans prescribed for it; upon its completion he brings into it his family and attendants, together with every species of animal;

the flood continues for six days and nights, until all mankind is destroyed; the flood then subsides, the ark settles upon Mount Nisir, and Ut-napishtim releases successively a dove, a swallow, and a raven, the latter of which, upon finding that the waters had quite subsided, " ate and croaked and did not return," whereupon Ut-napishtim leaves the ark and in thanksgiving offers a sacrifice to the gods, who in great delight gather " like flies " about it. There are so many points of contact here with the Hebrew story that the latter can scarcely be anything other than a Hebrew edition of the Babylonian. . . .

This paper is not intended to present an exhaustive survey of all the instances of foreign influence in the literature of the Old Testament. That would require a book of large proportions. Enough has been said, however, to indicate that the character of the Old Testament literature does illustrate the interpenetration of cultures in the ancient world. Indeed, one might infer from the study that the Hebrews got all their culture from other peoples; but that, of course, is not true. Their relation to others is like that of Shakespeare to his predecessors. " He took their materials and transformed them by the touch of his immortal genius. He borrowed indiscriminately on every hand, but he made what he borrowed forever his own by the magic of his skill and the grandeur of his matchless style." So likewise did the Hebrews. Whatever they may have borrowed they made their own, they ethicized and sublimated, so that no contemporary literature is at all comparable to theirs. In them, as so often, the pupil surpassed the teacher.

CULTURE CONTACTS AND SYNCRETISM

The Early Period of Christianity. — The time of the opening of the Christian Era was one of pronounced syncretization. Greece, Macedonia, Egypt, Syria, Persia, and Palestine were all mingling in a way which gave ample opportunity for assimilation, each from the other. Under the hand of Rome, with its shifting of populations in trade, war, travel, and study, the whole world, thus governed, became acquainted with what was best and worst everywhere else.

The culture of the Empire became an eclectic one. Nothing was " pure " in the original sense. The faithful men of each old tradition regretted that that which was precious to them had been diluted. The Greek language and letters were vulgarized. The old Roman gods were in transition. The philosophies of Greece had been " warmed " by the incoming of Eastern tides of thought. The dramatic and ecstatic aspects of the Mysteries were giving place to more measured and semi-rationalized forms of worship.

The advent of Christianity was an added feature of this mingling of differing ideas and ideals. In all other aspects of the movement it had been " give and take." With Christianity it was to fare no differently. One of the most difficult problems in the history of the first three centuries of the Christian Era is the attempt to tell what was derived from Christianity by the culture and religions of this time. Resemblances in doctrine and ideals can be accounted for in at least four ways: (1) They are from Christianity, and taken over by the older culture and religion. (2) They were assimilated by Christianity from its environment. (3) Both got it from some common older source. (4) Resemblances sprang up independently, in each group. Doubtless there is some truth in each contention. It seems improbable, however, that there could have been a very large contribution on the part of the Christian movement to its contemporaries. It was relatively small, and, being new, was itself in process of formation. The number of Christians going from the Church into the other faiths was negligible, and other influences probably did not accomplish much in transference in this direction.

The place where we come upon ground which is quite

certain is the relation of Gnosticism to Christianity. Harnack has called Gnosticism " the acute Hellenization of Christianity." Certain of its sects might also well be called "the acute Christianization of Hellenism." The Gnostic thinkers found a group of concepts in Christianity which were easily usable, and they moved into the Christian group, feeling that they had discovered true kinsmen. Such terms as Pater, Charis, Nous, Zoe, Aletheia, Ecclesia, Paracletos, Pistis, Elpis, Agape, Sophia, Christos, Pneuma Hagion, and others were the stones of which the bridge across from one to the other was built. Doubtless at first the Christians were delighted to have so fine an indorsement from so scholarly and eminently respectable a class. Later they found to their consternation that these people who were in the church and who were using the Christian Scriptures (as well as offering some of their own) were undermining the whole Christian structure.

When we come to consider the culture which came across from the environing religions to Christianity, again we are in difficulty, for almost any proposition can either be located in Judaism, and therefore derived from it as an orthodox source, or else regarded as a " logical consequent " of some earlier Christian faith, and therefore acquired by independent rather than by assimilative processes.

Christianity had a very rapid growth. Its increase, after the first generation, was almost wholly from Gentile sources. These Gentiles were not without religious connections before becoming converted to Christianity. Coming into the Christian movement, and making use of words and ideas which were common both to their old faith and to Christianity, they would, by reason of their old habit, give to any term a meaning as much in common with their old view as with the new. There are very many standard features of early Christianity which were either taken from these other religions, or else being already present were caused to grow and flourish under the influence of the new convert with his relish for these things.

To attempt to illustrate: It is doubtful if the doctrine of the Trinity would have been definitely formulated if Christianity had stayed in its early Palestinian environment. The worship of Christ as God would possibly have been established with difficulty on Palestinian soil. The ideas of new birth, of mystical union with the Deity, of revelation (in the sense of Gnosis), of the sacramental value of the memorial meal and of the ritual washing, of blood-redemption, of the " Mother of God," of a celibate sanctity above that of other mortals, of the flesh as the dwelling-place, or occasion of sin — these were certainly all heightened by contact with contemporary pagan religions, and by reason of similar ideas in those religions made the transition for those converted to Christianity an easy matter.

Christians in response to, and under the tutelage of, a Gentile environment evolved an interpretation of religious experience along the lines and in the language of the thought-world which constituted for Gentiles the realm of greatest reality. (Case, *Environment of Early Christianity*, 189-90.)

Christianity came to put stress upon the chief values which the pagan religions had been seeking to inculcate. It, like them, was a religion of redemption, but with a Savior more truly historical, and with evidences of achievement much stronger than the other religions of mythical dying-and-rising gods.

In the meantime, the action and interaction of the pagan faiths tended to give comprehensiveness.

Their union constituted a pantheistic religion of the deified world. From coarse fetichism and savage superstition the learned priests of the Asian cults gradually produced a system of metaphysics and eschatology. . . . This religion was no longer like that of ancient Rome, a mere collection of propitiatory and expiatory rites performed by citizens for the good of the state; it pretended to offer to all men a world conception which gave rise to a rule of conduct and placed the end of existence in a future life. It was more unlike the worship which Augustus had sought to strengthen than the Christianity against which he had contended. The two opposed creeds moved in the same intellectual level and moral sphere, and one could actually pass from the one to the other without any great shock or interruption. . . . The Roman aristocracy, which had remained faithful to the gods of their ancestors, did not have a mentality or morality very different from that of Christianity of their time. The religious and mystical spirit of the Orient had slowly overcome the social organism, and prepared all nations to unite in the bosom of a universal church. (Cumont, *Oriental Religions in Roman Paganism*, 210—211.)

The syncretism of the first three centuries had so worked its way through the pagan faiths, on the one hand, and so fully colored the Christian religion, on the other, that it was no great change in the Roman Empire when Christianity became a state religion and the people of the Empire were expected to conform.

CULTURE PATTERN AND THE BORROWING PROCESS

A tacit assumption of Christian missionary endeavor among pre-literate peoples has been that Christianity would be beneficial to any people who could be induced to embrace it. As a corollary stands the high light of missionary hope, that those whom it is sought to convert may become in habits and ideals as nearly as possible identical with the missionaries themselves, as a Christian type. The possibility of such a change assumes two processes — the renunciation by the non-Christian peoples of their native religion and social organization and the adoption by these peoples of Christian culture and social organization. A study of the actual process of religious acculturation is suggestive as an indication of the general process which works itself out when two groups with well systematized, but highly dissimilar, social organizations chance to meet on a common area.

Some of the material used in this paper applies to a time when misunderstanding of preliterate peoples was even greater than at present. The lack of knowledge concerning the preliterates resulted in the failure to recognize that the preliterates already had a well-developed social organization, into which the activities of the individual members of the group fitted with exact nicety and through which their ideals and desires found adequate expression. While this lack of appreciation of cultural organization has been somewhat modified by the work of anthropologists, there is still prevalent a notion that a people will discard in its entirety its traditional culture and whole-heartedly accept a dissimilar culture. A study of actual situations seems to indicate that instead of a complete substitution of a new culture for an old, the process consists of the mutilation of the old culture to permit elements of the new to enter, the result being a fusion of the two into a third type of culture. This method of adjustment seems especially apt to occur when the invading culture is more complex and abstract than the native culture, as has been the case in the contacts of European with preliterate culture.

For purposes of illustration, the situation of the Indians and Eskimos in North America has been chosen as both recent and immediate. Among the Indians the early contacts with the whites were of two kinds, with the pioneering traders and settlers and with the missionaries. The pioneer, with his eager eyes turned toward the promise of the West, saw in the Indian an impediment to his own interests. The unbroken succession of Indian wars with the inevitable last word by the whites in the shape of a final massacre, the later treaties which restricted the territory of the Indians, the final herding of the Indians on reservations, tell of the " conflict of wishes "that characterized the frontier interaction of whites and Indians, with the whites inevitably successful through their superior numbers and technique, the Indians defiant, but helpless. The second class of whites, the missionaries, regarded the Indian as a soul to be saved, but whose saving was worth all the hazards of the frontier.

The history of Eskimo and white contacts differs somewhat from that of the Indians and whites. The same two classes of whites (traders and missionaries) found their way among the Eskimos of Greenland in the eighteenth century and at a somewhat later date on the mainland of North America. However, the bitter cold was not conducive to extensive colonizing and the pressure of the whites on the Eskimos for land is in no way comparable to the situation among the Indians. Moreover, the Indians were accustomed to fighting among their own tribes, while war has no place in the Eskimos' repertory of reactions. In general, however, the reactions of the Eskimos to Christianity corroborate the conclusions reached from the study of the Indians.

It is well at the outset to gain some general conception of Indian and Eskimo religion and social organization. The religion of the American Indian had two aspects, one concerning the individual, the other the group. In the individual aspect the belief in a magic power dominated. This power, unlike the Christian deities, was not personified in a supernatural individual or individuals, but might be found in animals, men, inanimate objects, or deities. This belief was widespread among the Indians and it was this indefinite, but powerful, magic which constituted the Manito of the Algonquian, the Wakanda of the Sioux, the Orenda of the Iroquois, the Sullia of the Salish, Naualak of the Kwakiutl, and the Tamanoas of the Chinook. Sickness, misfortune, death, were attributed to the influence of this magic power. Notwithstanding the strength of this power over the affairs of man, the Indians believed it could be controlled and its good-will retained through various rules of conduct, such as taboos of food, work, behavior on special occasions, and also through magical practices, such as incantations, prayers, charms or fetishes, prayer-sticks, offerings, and sacrifices. The fundamental concept of a supernatural power is similar to that of the Christian religion, differing, however, in not being localized in well-defined deities. The methods of retaining the favor of the supernatural power are not unlike those of the Christian religion and were of a character to cause both Catholicism and Protestantism to make an appeal to the Indians. The taboos of conduct were favorable to Protestantism with its careful questioning of individual conduct, while the mystical practices were similar to the ceremonial symbolism of the Catholic church.

But in addition to the individual aspect of religion the Indian's social structure was religious in character. The rites of puberty, the sun dance of the Plains Indians, the secret societies of the Pacific Coast Indians, were religious and pertained to the welfare of the tribe as a whole. Moreover, the religious beliefs, myths, and social organization within each tribe tended to support one another and to form a structural unity. The Indians were carefully taught the traditions and customs of their tribe and suffered penalties, actual or magical, for transgressing the ancestral customs. The stringency with which the individual was held in the accustomed ways is without a parallel in modern civilized life. The Indian could not leave his tribe without being at the mercy of other tribes; his very existence depended upon conformity to the group regulations. Moreover, however strange the practices of the Indians may seem to those of another culture, they were carefully controlled and recognized as proper; hence they did not lead to degeneration of the individual.

The native Eskimo religion was similar to that of the

Indians. The Eskimos believed in a number of supernatural beings called " inua " or owners who had power over the actions and well-being of men. These spirits might be controlled in turn by certain charms and taboos and through the operations of the *shamans* or *angakoks*. There was also a widespread belief in certain mythical characters, chiefly Tornarsuk, the chief of the spirits, and Sedna, a woman who controlled the animals used for food. The social organization was loose in character, each village being an independent unit, with an advisory headman, whose position was not well enough defined for him to be called a chief. Enforcement of the law and customs rested on the individual, blood revenge being commonly practiced. In the family life, monogamy, polyandry, and polygamy were all common. Infanticide, killing of orphans and the aged were accepted modes of behavior when there was no one to care for the dependent individual — cases in which the welfare of the group took precedence over the life of the individual.

The early missionaries did not so much misunderstand the native religion as fail utterly to see that there was any religion or social organization among the preliterates. The following excerpts from the records of the Spanish fathers in California are illustrative.

" The different tribes by no means represented communities of rational beings, who submit to laws and regulations and obey their superiors, but resembled nothing less than a herd of swine, each of which runs about grunting as it likes, together today and scattered tomorrow,till they meet again by accident at some future time. In a word, the Californians lived as though they were freethinkers, *salva venia*, materialists."

As for the mental capacity of the Indians: " We proceed very slowly with these poor savages because of their remarkable dullness to learn and to make themselves capable of grasping the sublime mysteries of our holy faith."

The attitude of the missionaries was the very natural result of the yet unshaken faith in one absolute and true religion, which should in time prevail over all the world, and of the limited knowledge concerning preliterate peoples. The missionaries clearly saw their duty to be the reconstruction of the preliterates along the lines of European culture. In their efforts to force upon Indian and Eskimo the European God, they defined the native gods in terms of Christianity, which meant that at best the native god became synonymous with the devil and at worst was altogether annihilated. Thus Venegas, in a book published in 1758, based on missionary records, speaks of the Indian " priests " who attempted in the native culture to control supernatural powers which are referred to by Venegas as " apostate spirits " or " even the devil himself." Tornarsuk, the chief Eskimo spirit, was identified with the Christian devil by the missionaries, and the woman who controlled the food animals became the grandmother of the devil.

Since the native spirits became allies of the devil, from the missionary point of view all ceremonies pertaining to the native religion were an offense to the true God of Christianity, and in fact any custom not similar to Christian customs came to be regarded as part and parcel of heathenism and hence to be eradicated as rapidly as possible. The efforts of the missionaries were direct and to the point. Tribal customs were thrown aside, and new ways were instituted, partly by rewards of food and blankets for uniting with the Christian church, partly by threats and force when compliance was not given.

But the natives' lives were deeply grounded in their own culture, and they could not suddenly be forced into a new culture and given a new point of view. Every people reads into its religion, spontaneously accepted, its hopes and aspirations, attributes to its deity power to fulfil those hopes, and in its religion finds expression for the wishes that have not come to full bloom in actuality. Through their native religion the Indians found a more or less satisfactory adjustment to the ragged edges of their life and idealization of the group values. The Christian religion was to them a foreign religion, connected in no way with the problems they had to meet nor with the traditional values and codes of behavior of the tribe. The Christian religion came to them, moreover, as a repressive measure. With it went the restriction of their territory, the obliteration of ancestral ceremonies, sacred and beloved by the tribe, the defining of their gods as devils, confinement and corporal punishment for disobedience to the church ordinances, hideous wars and loss of life. It is true that the native religion was not retained intact in the face of the direct action of the missionaries. But the result was not, as the missionaries had hoped, the remaking of the Indians into European Christians. Religious beliefs and practices which incorporated traces of both Christianity and the native tribal culture replaced the Indian religion; for convenience in discussion, these blended beliefs may be classified as the survival of native beliefs and customs; interpretations of Christianity by the natives in the light of native culture; sporadic revivals of native culture and the formation of " new religions."

Survival of Native Beliefs and Customs. — The survival of ancestral beliefs and customs, while significant in itself as an indication of the tenacity with which deeply rooted habits of generations cling, is also the groundwork of the two other phenomena mentioned above. Repressed by the missionaries, the subterranean stream of tribal tradition was still operative in controlling the Indians and ready to break forth on the surface with the first release of external pressure.

The California Indians illustrate this point well. Missions were established in California by the Spanish fathers in the middle of the eighteenth century. The California Indians were peaceful and made little resistance to the aggressions of the Spaniards. The Spanish fathers, in addition to attempting to teach the Indians the prayers, church ritual, and doctrines, also gathered the Indians into settlements of from a few hundred to several thousand and taught them agriculture and trades, gave them food and clothing, and encouraged them to give up their tribal customs. The Indians made few protests and such protests as they made were unsuccessful. Refusal to work was met by refusal of food; disobedience, by confinement or corporal punishment; escape, by pursuit and capture. The only rebellion of any note occurred at the San Diego mission a few years after it was founded and resulted in the loss of only a few lives. In 1834 (after some seventy years of direct missionary influence) the Mexican government secularized the missions and divided among the Indians all the land and herds which had been held in trust for them by the missionaries, and the Indians were free from the restrictions imposed upon them by the missionaries.

While the missionaries were yet in the field, the following ceremonies and customs are known to have persisted among the Indians at least up to 1811, in spite of the ardent efforts of the missionaries to eradicate them.

1. The worship of a bird variously recorded at the mission stations as a vulture, eagle, bird resembling a kite, raven. The bird in question was caught while young, confined, carefully and plenteously fed and when fat killed and its body burned, while the Indians threw seeds, beads, and other articles on the fire. The symbolism of the ceremony was apparently unknown to the fathers.
2. Cremation of the dead with ceremony. At some of the mission stations this custom was discontinued.
3. Infanticide.

More significant is the fact that while the Spanish

fathers were toiling so earnestly to convert the -Indians, a strange native missionary enterprise was also taking place, by which a native religion was extended from the north to the tribes under the control of the missionaries and disseminated among the proteges of the Spaniards.

The evidence seems clear that the Indians found in their native religions more satisfaction than in Christianity with all its attendant depreciation of tribal culture and its irritating restrictions.

With the Eskimos, the case is not so clear-cut, since the missionaries are still in the field and since relationships have not been so tense between the natives and the whites as with the Indians. As Christianity is still constantly before the Eskimos, they are nominally Christians, although they retain at the same time parallel native beliefs, but on a lower scale. The native spirits are believed to live in the interior parts of the country or to roam through the air and to be angry with the Eskimos for turning from them to the Christian gods. In like manner the Christian heaven has been added to the spiritual worlds already conceived by the Eskimos. There seems to the Eskimo to be nothing incompatible in this cumulative religion; the missionaries have brought to the Eskimos new knowledge but this fact does not displace their previous knowledge.

The Indians, no doubt because of their greater friction with the whites, tended to reject Christianity, whereas the Eskimos accept and respect it, but retain their native religion on a lower level.

Interpretations of Christianity in the Light of Tribal Culture. — Interesting and significant are the interpretations placed upon Christianity by the Indians and Eskimos. The Indian can do nothing more with Christianity than view it through the pattern which training and experience have placed in his mind. There is no miraculous way by which the missionary, try as he will, can implant into the Indian mind his own idea of Christianity, bulwarked about as it is by all the ideals, taboos, and proprieties, which we lump under the term of Christian civilization. The Indian has been subjected to training as severe in its power to mold the organization of thought and to establish a point of view as the white man, differ though it may from Christian training; and it is from a background of this tribal culture that he interprets Christianity. Engelhardt relates the experience of one father at Saint Francis Xavier mission about 1700 who tried to impress upon the Indians the hideous-ness of the fire and pain of hell. Later he heard the Indians say to each other that hell was a better land than the earth, for in hell there was always a sufficient supply of wood and one would not need to go cold. It is significant of the attitude of the missionaries that the Indians' comments were attributed to the " extreme dullness of the poor natives."

In many cases the misinterpretation did not involve merely a misconception of a Christian concept but a mixture of Christian and Indian beliefs. In this class comes the identifying of a native god or spirit with the Christian devil, a practice furthered by many missionaries in their effort to displace the native spirits in favor of the Christian deities. Thus Towish, originally meaning spirit (as when a man dies, he becomes Towish) has been identified with the devil, and in fear the Indians have devised songs and charms as a form of exorcism. These practices are modern and grow out of the attributing to a native spirit the characteristics of the Christian devil.

In a similar fashion the early missionaries found upon their return to the cross which they had erected and left, that it had been adorned with arrows, sticks, feathers, fish, meat, and clams; they were told by the Indians that the cross had been illuminated at night and had increased in size until it reached the heavens and that the offerings were to propitiate the Christian symbol that it might not harm them. In this case the Christian symbol was endowed by the Indians with magical power, and tribal methods were used to control it.

Many incidents might be recited of the manner in which the Eskimos interpret the Protestant taboos, particularly the prohibition of work on the Sabbath. One of the principal sources of food is the whale. The whaling season is only six weeks long and the Eskimos expect to catch enough during the brief period of the annual whale migration to supply their needs. But after they became Christians nothing could induce them to go out in their boats on Sunday. Consequently they lost most of Saturday afternoon drawing in their boats and most of Monday morning in preparing to put the boats out, in addition to Sunday, from the all too short whaling season. In vain the local missionary expostulated with them. Their reply was that they dared not work on Sunday and that since God controlled the whales and the winds and since the missionary was his messenger, the missionary's duty was plainly to see to it that God did not bring disaster upon them.

The old taboos of the Eskimos in their tribal culture carried a magical penalty of misfortune or death for disobedience. The tribaltaboos were true collective ideas (collective representation) and were accepted without question by the Eskimos. The taboos taught by the missonaries have been accepted in the same spirit, as commands to be in plicitly obeyed, the penalty being eternal damnation, regardless of what the material loss may be for obedience.

In like manner, the faith of the Eskimos in the power of the *shaman* has been transferred to the missionary, who is expected to control storms and wind by appeals to God. He is not merely a teacher, but the spokesman of God. Prayers are believed to have unlimited power. Inone village the Eskimos had a " caribou prayer," brought from a mission station, which guaranteed a good catch of caribou.

In the persistence of native beliefs and the misinterpretations of Christianity, there is a fusion of the two strains of religion which enables the Eskimo to retain the structure of his world as he conceives it and yet to incorporate into his philosophy the new religion brought by the missionaries. Tannaumirk, a Mackenzie River Eskimo, stated that he could understand how Christ could raise people from the dead, for he had seen one of the native *shamans* accomplish this feat, although the white people could scarcely be expected to believe in Christ's power, since none of their own countrymen were able to do such things. In addition to this comparison of Christian tradition with Eskimo tradition, there is a substitution of Christian deities for native spirits without any material change in the relationship of the individuals to the spirits. Thus where the *shaman*, the native spiritual leader and adviser, was taught songs and spells by the man in the moon, now the deacons in the Eskimo church learn hymns and chants (which Stefansson says are in the jargon language used by the whalers) from St. Peter during visits by the Eskimos to heaven.

The conclusion which one draws from the foregoing discussion is not that the Indians and Eskimos are incapable of understanding and appreciating Christian principles, but that the Christian forms and symbols, which tend in time to gain the major emphasis, are the outgrowth of a type of culture which has little real application to the Indian's or Eskimo's mode of life. The situation has been further complicated by the failure of the missionaries to recognize a well-developed native culture and by efforts to effect a rapid change in both material culture and point of view. The Indians and Eskimos very naturally cling to the customs which have come down to them from numberless generations and about which their myths are built. Yet with all the tenacity of tribal customs, they have exhibited a marked adaptation to Christian customs and religious beliefs, among the Indians particularly after the period of frontier wars had passed. There is a distinct deviation from Christianity, however, in the retention of certain native ceremonies and favorite spirits, in the re-interpretation of Christianity in the light of tribal culture, and in the successful efforts to establish an independent Indian church, modeled in part on the Christian church but sufficiently Indian to give the feeling of ownership and leadership and to incorporate the Indian's own ideals for his progress and future life.

AN ORIENTAL VIEW OF CULTURE CONTACTS

Rightly or wrongly, the East has come to think of Christianity as part of the political game of the West. In religion it talks of " going about doing good "; in politics this takes the form of " ruling others for their good." Has the East reasonable grounds for thinking so?

Let us look at China through Eastern eyes. She has been in continuous contact with organized Christianity for about three hundred and fifty years. Her early relations were most friendly; she undoubtedly found many of the missionaries to be sincere men, who had given up the comforts of " civilized " countries to dwell among " backward " peoples and to save their " heathen " souls from perdition. But the tragedy of the situation lies in the fact that foreign governments have frequently followed the path which the missionary had blazed. Where the missionary finds his field of activity, there the Chinese finds — not infrequently — the fixed bayonets of a foreign power.

The killing of a missionary, whether it be due to his own indiscretion, to the anti-foreign fury of some Chinese zealot, or to some other cause, has often been used by his government as an occasion for making demands for concessions from the Chinese Government. Chinese diplomatic history will furnish many examples of this kind. The Boxer war of 1900 was an evidence that the Chinese were weary of such frequent interference and were willing no longer to be oppressed by foreigners. And what was the result? The Chinese Government had to pay an indemnity amounting to $320,000,000; besides this she had also to yield ' the important right of tariff autonomy. Similarly she lost most of her valuable seaports. Studying the history of their ancient land, the young patriots see how closely the expansion of the " spheres of influence "of foreign powers has been connected not only with the intrigue and wirepulling of commercial and political interests, but also with the killing of foreign missionaries by would-not-be-saved Chinese rebels. Thus, indeed, the patriotic feeling to rid China of the missionary pestilence was aroused.

The anti-Christian movement, while it admits that to a large extent the incentive, both for the missionaries and for those who back them up financially, has been religious belief, seeks to show to the thinking public how frequently the presence of the missionaries and the effects of their work have been taken advantage of by governments and traders, just as the missionaries have too often profited by privileges which could be claimed by citizens of foreign powers. The whole history of the relations of the Western nations to China reveals a long series of encroachments on China's sovereign rights. So much so, that Mr. Dennett very aptly remarks, " These Chinese were free to abstain from Christianity, as from opium, but they were not free to prohibit them." Why? Simply because brute force and not the principle of right had given the Western powers the title to interfere with China's sovereign rights. If there were no treaties of Nanking, Tientsin, and Shimo-noseki, if there were no Boxer protocols and demands and concessions, the attitude of young China toward Western Christianity would have been, if less friendly than it was in its early contacts, at least not as hostile as it is today.

The feeling in India is not very different; it is the

common belief that the Bible comes first and then the gunpowder. Wherever the Christians go, says the Hindu, they somehow manage to meddle with the political .. rights of the people. Before the Christians went to Africa the Africans had lands but no Bibles; now they have Bibles but no lands. In Kenya, for instance, the poor helpless natives are being driven out of all their desirable and fertile lands. Under the Lands Act of 1913, eighty-eight per cent of the land of the South African Union was reserved for the white men, leaving twelve per cent for the five million black men, who are four times as numerous. Again in Kenya we find that of the good land available six thousand square miles have been allotted under a system of " Reserves," giving no permanent but only an indefinite tenure, so that it may be said that the Africans there have no legal rights whatever to their own native land. Hence the East concludes that the political method of the West is first to send missionaries, then traders, and then gunboats to deprive the helpless peoples of their lands and to take possession of their natural resources.

Is it any wonder if, with such knowledge of Western penetration, the East becomes distrustful of the professed philanthropy of the Christian, turns hostile to a religion which has let itself be used by foreign powers for political expansion, and grows more and more suspicious of the real mission of the missionary?

Rightly or wrongly even today the missionaries are frequently thought of as the " political agents " of alien governments. Does the missionary allow himself to be so mistaken by the East?

To be more specific, let us take the case of an American missionary in India. Having signed the declaration and having been duly recommended by the Conference, he is sent out to India. There he is to consider himself the guest of the British Government. His schools are inspected by the

Government agent; his work is visited in a most friendly way by the Governor of the state or province. He frequently receives Government aid for the maintenance of the mission school and for the erection of new buildings. In return for all these and in accordance with his declaration, he holds himself responsible for the behavior of the pupils and of the teachers in the schools of which he is in charge. He is expected, of course, to be careful to do or say nothing which would render the working of the British Government in India more difficult. These regulations and guest-relationships very seriously influence the work and attitude of the missionary, to an extent to which he himself is not fully aware. He believes he is neutral; but under the conditions of his declaration is real neutrality possible?

The missionary is thus placed in a false position and is subjected to very serious accusations. The British Government has a ruling that no student should take part in politics, though at present it is not quite so strict as it used to be. In a certain town a political meeting was held in the courtyard of a temple, and the missionary principal of the school was expected to keep the boys from going to the meeting. Some of the young enthusiasts attended the meeting and the missionary securing their names reported them to the local Government School Inspector. Immediately the news spread that the missionary was a spy of the alien government and that instead of training patriotic citizens to live for the country and work for its emancipation, he was trying to develop " slavish mentality " in the pupils and to promote loyalty to the British Government. In such cases the missionary appears to the non-Christian as a political agent masquerading under a religious cloak.

The fear is also widespread, and not without reason, that Western Christianity tends to suppress not only national aspirations but also national cultures. The normal thing for any country is to promote its ' national culture and preserve its race experience; but when it is inter- fered with by a foreign institution, either in the form of a government or a mission, then the national culture suffers. In India, for instance, the British Government introduced Western education but pledged itself not to interfere with the religions of the people and left that field of activity to the missionaries of the West. The Hindus attribute the decay of Indian national culture largely to the fact that, on the one hand, the British Government has refused to encourage it under the pretense of non-interference with religions and, on the other hand, the missionary enthusiasts by their fanatical intolerance have attempted, not simply to ignore it as has the Government, but positively to destroy it. Not being " Christian," it was " heathen," according to the missionary, and hence preordained to damnation!

The East is thankful for the introduction of Western education, but it resents its introduction at the expense of national cultures. Making English the medium of instruction results, as was the case in Ireland, in intellectual deterioration and social disintegration. The missionaries have not only despised our literature but have also condemned our music and art, because they are connected with " heathen " religions. Their intolerance of everything which in any way savored ofheathenism has been so great that, in India for instance, they have not allowed their converts to retain their Hindu names. This would explain how it happens that some Indians have such names as the author's, Joseph Gabriel, Mary McFarland, Henry Senecafalls, etc.

The Westernizing process is not confined to India. The anti-Christian movement of China similarly accuses Christianity of being a Western-' izing force. The mission schools are accused of having grossly neglected to emphasize Chinese culture and literature. This charge is substantiated by the fact that as a rule graduates of mission schools are woefully lacking in a knowledge of Chinese literature and in an ability to express themselves in correct Chinese. Let us suppose that the children of some of the schools in the state of New Jersey were taught Confucianism as the best code of morals; the geography, not of New Jersey and the United States, but of Manchuria, Peking, Canton, etc.; the history, not of the United States, but of the Chinese Dynasties and the Republic; let us suppose that they were taught a little English but much of Chinese, that they were trained to write Chinese with ease and to speak it with fluency; and that the whole system of education was based not on the American philosophy of education and pedagogy but on the Chinese. Would you say that these schools were training the young to take their places as intelligent citizens of the American republic?

Even though such an education were financed by Chinese capital and carried on with a purely philanthropic motive, would not Americans revolt against such an un-American system of education? Would not the American Government be justified if it required the registration of all the schools for American children conducted by the Chinese, and if it legislated in such a way that in course of time these schools would become American in the personnel of their administrative staff, in their supporting constituencies and legal relationships, in the content of their curricula, and above all in their entire atmosphere? This is exactly what the anti-Christian movement wants to do with all the schools conducted by the missions for the Chinese children. It wants these schools, instead of being Westernizing and denationalizing centers, to become radiating centers for a higher nationalism fitting in with the whole educational structure. Not a wicked ambition, is it? Hence it is that the Chinese Government requires the registration of all mission schools.

The Chinese Christian Community, much like the Indian Christian Community referred to elsewhere, tends to become isolated from the rest of the people. In China the right to preach throughout the empire and the protection of law for their lives and property, were given to the missionaries as a result of concessions wrung from the Chinese Government by foreign powers. The American Treaty with China, Article 14, has a clause which reads thus: "Any person, whether citizen of the United States or Chinese convert, who according to these tenets peaceably teaches and practices principles of Christianity, shall in no case be interfered with or molested therefor."

Such agreements placed the Chinese Christians under the protection of foreign powers. Even some incorrigible criminals became Christians nominally in order to escape lawful punishment. It was only as the protector of the faith of the converts, to be sure, that a foreign power could intervene legally, but in practice the result was to separate the Chinese Christian from the mass of his fellow-countrymen and sometimes to help criminals to evade the law. Such treaties dealt a serious blow to the prestige and sovereignty of the Chinese State, as they resulted practically in removing the Chinese Christians from its jurisdiction.

The political complications of Christianity, much as we may regret it, have brought about the inevitable consequence — animosity. The political and commercial penetration of the West has engendered a new spirit in the East. The rising tide of nationalism, as it is called, is not a desire to be aggressive but a longing to be free to determine its own destiny and to live naturally and normally within its own boundary unhampered by foreign interference. Western Christianity, according to the present temper of the East, has been philanthropic in profession but political in action. It is compelled not to further the national aspirations of the people but to exert its influence in the interests of alien governments. The Eastern will to be free and its passionate desire to throw off all foreign domination have begun, therefore, to make themselves felt in the domain of religion also.

Along with the political imperialism of the West, the religious imperialism of Christianity has added much to arouse the spirit of hostility in the East. The religious hospitality of the Orient is due to the recognition that while there is only one God, there are many approaches to him. The Hindu would say that just as the many rivers which swell by raindrops empty themselves into one mighty ocean, so also the devotees of all religions, enriched by their various religious experiences, find their way to the bosom of the One Infinite Being. But a Christian does not seem to look at it that way, and the attempt of the missionary appears to be to make Christianity the Nordic among religions. Perhaps the Semitic background of Christianity is responsible to a large extent for its exclusiveness. " Thou shalt have no other gods before me ... for I the Lord thy God am a jealous God," said the Semite. Coupled with the intemperate aggressiveness of the Western nations, the simple religion of the humble Nazarene has become the most aggressive, exclusive, and powerfully organized religion in the world. The Nordic-complex in religion shows itself clearly in all Christian literature. Take for instance, the hymn " From Greenland's Icy Mountains " and go through verse after verse; it will surprise one that such hymns are found in Christian hymnals. Glance at some of the lines:

The *heathen* in his blindness
Bows down to wood and stone.
Shall *we*, whose souls are *lighted*
With *wisdom* from on high,
Shall *we* to men *benighted*
The lamp of life deny?

Notice the striking Christian modesty in this hymn, composed by a bishop! Another Christian, like Bishop Heber, is Kipling of immortal fame. He sings thus:

Ship me somewheres east of Suez,
Where the best is like the worst;
Where there ain't no ten commandments
And a man can raise a thirst.

It never occurred to him that the ten commandments were not the creation of his forefathers and that they really had their origin " east of Suez." In fact, it is the East which has given all the great religions of today, not excluding Christianity.

In order to establish the superiority of Christianity the missionaries had to write volumes on the differences between religions. No one will question the fact that all missionary literature is for definite ends. The object of such writers has been to show the superiority of Christianity by giving it a background of the horrors of the " heathen " religions, to arouse an interest in the missionary enterprise by portraying the " unspeakable " immorality and evils of non-Christian societies, and finally to make the reader an enthusiastic supporter for the enterprise, financially and otherwise.

Imagine for a moment what a picture India would have of America if most of what she knew of America were from the writings of workers in the slums, of the anti-saloonists, of the crime investigators, of the red-light district workers, and of other such good people! If such literature flooded the markets of India for a half century, nay even for a quarter of a century, it would be as impossible for an American in India to convince the people brought up on such literature that Americans do not marry only to divorce, that killing one another is not the pastime of Americans, and that banks exist in spite of robbery, as it is for an Indian in America to convince those brought up on missionary literature that girl babies are not thrown into the Ganges, that the people of India are not savages, that social evils are not the monopoly of the East.

Just as they paint the dark side of the East for the West, so they paint the brighter side of the West for the consumption of the East. But with the growth of cultural intercourse with the West, the East is discovering things for herself about the assumed superiority of the West. The present anti-Christian attitude is a challenge based on increasing firsthand knowledge of the failure of Christianity to influence the lives of Western peoples. In days of old it used to be said that the lives of Europeans who lived in the East were obstacles to the progress of Christianity out there. But today in the life of the West itself Christianity— to the Eastern observer — stands exposed and condemned.

The rapidly growing commercial intercourse and the opportunities for practical education bring a large number of Oriental sojourners to the West. Every year students are coming in ever-increasing numbers to American universities. There are now about two thousand students from China, about one thousand from Japan, two thousand from the Philippine Islands, and about three hundred from India. They come here to prepare themselves to be of some service and leadership in their homelands. They undoubtedly carry back impressions of the West. Are such impressions pro-Christian or anti-Christian? Some of the Oriental students have seen with their own eyes the ghastly sight of the Negro being riddled with bullets by angry mobs under a " civilized " administration. They understand a caste system fostered by religion as in India, but they do not understand a caste system opposed by the teachings of Jesus but upheld by the churches of the South. These and like experiences of un-Christian practices are broadcasted in the East, and the non-Christian sees in them a wide gulf between the teachings of Jesus and the practice of his professed followers. The Mohammedan, therefore, speaks of his religion as being much more practical and democratic; so also the Chinese upholds Confucianism as a livable code of morality, and the Hindu says that

Christianity being idealistic, the West is not prepared to pay the price for it, and hence that it is not of much use in daily life.

When Dr. C. W. Gilkey was in India last winter, as the Barrows Lecturer sent by the University of Chicago, he was told that the Hindus once thought of America as the land of Christian idealism and of opportunity, but that now they think of it as the land which insults the Hindus, excludes the Asiatics, and lynches the Negro. Now that the social evils of the West are being exposed in the Orient, the East is losing confidence in the religion of the West. How can an anti-Christian attitude be prevented if the Western Christians, in the face of such facts, claim exclusive superiority?

The East has not only seen how the missionary's religion falls short of practice in its homelands, but the incoming of such large numbers of students has helped it to see also how money is raised to carry on the Christian propaganda. The East has seen itself misrepresented, has seen how the darkest side of Eastern life is presented and how money is raised by appeal to pity and condescension. With the awakening of national pride the Eastern peoples are no longer willing to see their countries sold for a mess of pottage. The Orientals naturally revolt against an organized religion which for the sake of money to propagate itself so humiliates them in the eyes of others. Such methods adopted for the express purpose of raising money and for the justification of the missionary enterprise, have not helped the West and the East to mutual respect. Only an interpretation of the higher idealism of both countries will bring about good will.

7

SOCIAL CHANGE IN CHINA

AMERICANIZATION AND SOCIAL CHANGE IN CHINA

Two or three Greek temples, a few structures with traces of Gothic inspiration, and a miscellany of imitation warehouses and factory buildings stand on the campus of the Chinese government university in Nanking — an architectural hodgepodge worthy of an American state university. Half a mile away are a group of magnificent buildings with heavy black overhanging roofs curling skyward at the corners, carved banisters, and richly painted paneled ceilings, redolent of old China. They are the lovely Asiatic shell of a Christian mission college founded and supported by American Methodists.

That is typical. In fifty years the great port cities of China will have left hardly a trace of the lovely old Chinese architecture — except in the mission-college buildings and in the few joss temples which will doubtless be preserved to gratify the tourist trade. The foreign mission schools, hurriedly Chinafying themselves to meet the nationalist attack, are spending tens of thousands of dollars in adapting the old Chinese style to modern requirements. The sweeping green roofs and gaily painted beams of the Peking Union Medical College, built with Rockefeller money, are a joy to the eye. Nanking University and Ginling College for women near by are good to look upon. But in four months in China I saw only one beautiful recent building which did not owe its existence to foreigners—the Returned-Students' Club in Peking, a remodeled temple; and there the students may be suspected of having learned abroad their respect for old China.

Shanghai is a great British city, of solid British masonry; Tientsin is as foreign; even Canton, which has providentially escaped the curse of great foreign settlements, is enormously proud that Chinese have actually built a ten-story building on its Bund without foreign aid; and Canton's new buildings are as foreign to China as any suburb of Cleveland, Ohio, or Birmingham, England. Peking, a capital of politics rather than of commerce, resists the current most effectively.

You can buy Standard Oil kerosene in any village in China, and British-American cigarettes. The great corporations behind those products have in a generation taught the Chinese to change their habits in order to make them buy — the Standard Oil, indeed, used to give away lamps in order to create a market for the strange new fuel. If any third foreign product is on sale in the village it may well be Wrigley's chewing gum. I saw Spearmint gum on sale in the streets of Urga, the capital of Mongolia, 700 miles across the Gobi Desert from the most accessible railroad.

Architecture and chewing gum are outward symptoms of a profound inner change. Western architecture is spreading because it is cheaper. Gum and tobacco cost less than opium. Only American church-people can afford painted paneled ceilings and bright tile roofs with gargoyle corner ornaments. The Chinese — like the Europeans, like the whole world — are abandoning old beauties and old customs for cheaper and more efficient models. They are becoming modernized, standardized, Americanized, like Japan. Mystery, leisure, charm are ebbing; cost accounting is defeating tradition.

The cult of the efficient seems a matter of course to most Westerners and almost all Americans, but to the Chinese it is a revolution. Old " China-hands " will laugh at the suggestion that it has touched Chinese psychology — but old China-hands need a vacation and a perspective. The Chinese has for untold centuries followed tradition and has believed that it was wicked to deviate from it. His young men and young women are beginning to despise custom and tradition; and his middle-aged business men, almost unconsciously, are beginning to ignore it. It was only forty years ago that the first railroad tracks laid in China were torn up by superstitious officials; today they are an indispensable instrument of civil war, as is the once-despised telegraph. The only opposition to them comes from Westernized Chinese who know how easily international politics slip into an engineering contract. Once a contract is let, there is no longer much difficulty about arranging to remove the graves that beset all the short cuts. And a wanderer through the black lanes of an old Chinese city may be surprised to discover that the squeaky Chinese music that wails to the night is produced not by a stringed instrument but by a Victor record.

Foreign railroads, manners, oil, and architecture are prevailing because they are more efficient. American wheat, when it costs a dollar a bushel in Chicago, can be landed in Hankow, ten thousand miles away and six hundred miles up the Yangtze from Shanghai, cheaper than it can be brought from Shensi, only a thousand miles away, where it may sell for twenty-five cents. Railways and steamships make the difference; no wonder they and their products are breaking the crust of old China. Foreign clothes have made less progress because, in cold weather at least, they are less efficient than the old Chinese robes. Foreign hair-dressing

— including the bob — is making its way among the women. Curt foreign manners are replacing the leisurely old Chinese courtesy. The streets are being widened, and the intimacy of the old Chineseworkshop, opening on a narrow street and aware of all that its neighbors said and did, is disappearing. Foreign machinery is revolutionizing Chinese industry. Foreign ideas — and the railway, taking the young people away from their homes to study and to work — are breaking up the immobile unity of Chinese family life upon which the whole structure of Confucian ethics is based. Boys go away from home to study, and refuse to return to the wives of their parents' choice. In the port cities one meets sad young men who are homesick for New York, prefer fox-trotting to Mah Jong, and inquire eagerly about the Charleston.

Chinese, with their habit of explaining everything by thousand-year-old parallels, will tell you that there were student revolts in the Han dynasty, before Christ was born. The nationalism of the student movement today, however, passionately denouncing foreigners and all their works, is essentially a part of the cult of Western efficiency. This political nationalism, this conception of national sovereignty as a precious right to be cherished and preserved, has its roots in foreign education and practice — in part in Allied war-time propaganda. The old Chinese patriotism — a patriotism profounder than anything known in the West — was cultural rather than political, inclusive rather than exclusive. It was a loyalty to a civilization rather than to a state, conservative rather than aggressive. It was powerless to halt the intrusion of Western men and methods into the political and economic control of . China, and was satisfied because the Westerners were so obviously inferior in the refinements of living. The Chinese students of today belong to our flapper generation; flaunting their posters and banners, parading by thousands against the unequal treaties and making soap-box speeches about self-determination, they express contempt for the passivity of their elders. Theirs is not the language of old China but of the young West. When it defies us most violently young China is most certainly expressing its determination to be like us.

And this young China has a significance beyond its years. There are no middle-aged men in modern China. There are grand old men, survivals of the old regime; and young men, fresh from Western education. The old men cannot adapt themselves to the swirling changes; the young men are forced to act beyond their capacities. " It is unfortunate for men of talent to be born in China today," Hu Shih said to me once. " They get too far too easily; they are pushed rapidly to responsibilities beyond their powers — and they are done. Wellington Koo would have been a splendid permanent under-secretary of the Foreign Office — he becomes prime minister; Wu Pei-fu an excellent division commander — he has to try to be a generalissimo; two years after I returned from America a newspaper straw ballot declared me one of the twelve greatest living Chinese! When you have made a reputation you have to do one of two things: live up to it or live on it. In the first case, you are ruined physically; in the second, you are ruined morally and intellectually. You try to be a great man; you try to do too many things — and you break."

Boys out of college perforce assume jobs fit for men of mature years; college students do the work done in the West by men in their thirties; and mere high-school lads do a task of political agitation for which we would consider college men unripe. They do it badly enough, but there is no remedy; the twentieth century will not wait, and the work has to be done. The foreigners, safe in their compounds, complain that the boys are losing their schooling; but the students know that they are making a new China.

An old Chinese maxim said " Be old while you are young." In the West, Chen Tu-shu told his Peking students, we say " Stay young while you are growing old." Chen, like many Chinese, exaggerated our virtue, but it was a lesson old China needed. Without the iconoclastic students Sun Yat-sen's long yea"s of revolutionary activity would have been vain; the students poured their souls and blood ' the Second Revolution that seemed to fail in 1913; and it was the students of Peking who, in 1919, overturned a rotten and corrupt government, aroused a sodden nation and forced a surprised delegation at Paris to refuse to sign the Treaty of Versailles which confirmed Japan — for three short years — in possession of the sacred province of Shantung. It was a group of just returned students who, in the preceding two years, had laid the foundations of a greater revolution by exalting the spoken language of the people, decrying the artificiality of the old written language of the scholars, thus opening the way for a great germination of mass education. It was a student demonstration in Shanghai which silenced for a minute by police-guns, touched the spark that set the Chinese nation aflame in 1925 with a fire which is still scorching the proud British Empire. It is in the mere children who leave their classes for what seem futile patriotic parades that China's hope lies.

An Asiatic scholar, asked how the East could preserve its essential Orientalism while suffering industrialization, replied: "I don't think there is anything peculiarly Oriental and Occidental. There is merely medieval and modern." The great force which has maintained China's identity through fifty centuries is her worship of the past, but the mechanical superiority of the present has already proved its power to defy that ancient citadel. And as the other civilizations of antiquity crumbled when their beliefs decayed, so the old China is yielding to the new West. What happens in the port cities of China today will happen throughout China the day after tomorrow. The feverish, abnormal life of those cities has a significance out of all proportion to their share of

China's four hundred million people; the rest of China too will adopt the Western — or modern — method of working hectically while itworks, and of playing madly while it plays; it too will forget the Chinese — or medieval — knack of combining work and play so that long hours seem short. The port cities are a hint of China's tomorrow.

SOCIAL CHANGE, THE CHINESE FAMILY, AND WESTERN INDUSTRIALISM

Not until it encountered the Chinese family system, did industry meet an influence with which it could not cope. The Chinese proverb has it, " If a man leaves his village, he makes himself cheap ? goods leaving the village increase in value." This teaching, of course, while upholding the unity of the family, at the same time repudiated Western industrialism. Thus was prevented a national catastrophe. For had China welcomed industrialism hastily and enthusiastically, hundreds of capitalists would have withdrawn their money and energies from the handicraft industries for reinvestment in machines. Thousands upon thousands of older people, unfit to learn the new processes, would have been thrown out of employment. And in consequence, capitalists and laborers, equally ignorant of machine manufacture, would together have achieved colossal failure.

The family has been instrumental not only in protecting industry from itself, but in protecting the factories against the workers and the workers against the factories. Though the industrial workers are so low in the social scale that they feel family ties and family pressure less than do other classes, the family is still held, even in an industrial environment, jointly responsible for the acts of its members. If an operative steals and sells some imported rubber tubing. his family returns it to the factory and punishes the offender more severely than the law would have done. If a foreman takes advantage of his small authority to bully one of his operatives, the operative's family unite against the foreman and exert such pressure upon him that he is forced to give up a promising position. If a woman is inclined to be morally frivolous, the influence of her family acts as a restraint on her and as a guard for her against the male operatives and foremen.

The family promises to be of greatest use to industry through its ability to give clan support to workers on strike — especially against the foreign employer. The majority of the workers are miserably poor and completely dependent on their own efforts for their living; but many of them have come from the farms of the interior, and others, through endless gradations of relationship, are capable of drawing some of the most powerful clans to their aid. When the day arrives on which the workers unite in protesting against their living and working conditions, the employers cannot merely sit and wait for them to come back when their funds are exhausted. They will return to their families, and the union of thousands of clans in passive resistance can stop every industrial wheel in China. The seamen's strike in Hongkong gave forewarning. A general sympathetic strike resulted, and even the house " boys " left their kitchens. Canton cared for some hundreds of strikers, but the gilds and clans gave sums not easily overestimated.

Yet industry is breaking up the old family organization, with its scorn of new methods, new ideas, new authority, and is throwing the accent upon the individual rather than upon the group. It makes no difference to a cotton-mill whether it employs the second brother's wife, the third brother and the third sister, or whether it employs the women and leaves the men to enter trades or other factories. If industry knows that", under the old conventions, women and men were not allowed to work in the same room, it takes no account of that fact, but, with a mechanical disregard for social complications, assigns them to machines. Before the entrance of industry, the numerous heads under one roof in China usually belonged to one family. Now industry has drawn thousands into small areas and mingled the names of several clans in hopeless confusion within one doorway.

Naturally such arbitrary and radical changes in the working conditions must react on every phase of domestic life. Fifteen years ago China did not consider a woman respectable who worked outside her home. And existence there was spun over with a web of etiquette designed to reduce woman to complete subjection. She was strictly secluded in the woman's apartments and forbidden to speak to any man alone. During her life she observed the " three obediences." In youth she obeyed her father; married, she obeyed her husband; widowed, she obeyed her son. After death she spent eternity in obeying her husband. As heaven is to earth, so is man to woman, she was taught, and her life's motive was to live accordingly. Today there is still prejudice against women in industry. But it is less general, less venomous. Everyone acknowledges that women are in industry to stay.

The opportunity to earn more than sixty cents — Mexican, of course — a day is seldom offered to women outside the foreign factories with highly specialized machinery, bonuses, comparative charts and other devices to stimulate production and efficiency. The cotton-mills and the silk-filatures do not try to realize the ability of individual operatives. They employ their workers through labor contractors and their foremen, who secure enough operatives to attain the average production required each day or month. The usual wage for a beginner is from ten to fifteen cents a day. When she has acquired a certain skill, she is put on piece-work rates. Many factories, like the weaving-mills run by Chinese in the interior, allow the women to come three months without pay, to learn. At the end of that time they are either sent home or put on piece-work rates. Factories prefer to employ unmarried women because they do not have family demands to take them from their work, and because, the younger the girls, the more rapidly they learn and the more skillful they become within a certain period. Women who remain as unskilled workers receive from $8 to $10, Mexican, a month. The skilled worker may receive between $15 and $20. But forty cents a day is considered an excellent wage for a woman. A good forewoman will earn eighty cents a day. Some girls on exceedingly delicate work and some of the older forewomen are paid as much as $1 a day. These wages are, however, lower than would be given men for the same work.

Few factories have made any distinction, in employing women, between " big feet " and " little feet," although it is admitted that the " big feet " women are more efficient. Women with bound feet must have work that enables them to sit most of the time. Few of the young girls are thus handicapped unless already betrothed. In a certain factory not long since was a little girl of fourteen with such tiny feet that she could only sit on a stool and have her work brought to her. On inquiry it was found to be still possible to unbind her feet. Her parents were willing and she was more than eager, but her fiance refused his permission. He was a foreman in another factory and thought that the possession of a wife with such tiny feet would give him " face " among his associates. One factory, in order to discourage further foot-binding and to inspire the women to unbind the feet of their children, posted a notice that it would employ no new workers with bound feet. But it did. Everyone connived to defeat such an innovation. Women with bound feet were slipped into vacant places and said to be former employees, returning. Some new applicants wound their feet and wore large shoes. The notice disappeared. So did the new ruling.

Women as well as men may have to pay a *cutnshaw* of

a few *cash* or a copper to the gateman of the factory every morning. And women as well as men who secure their places through a contractor must pay him a definite percentage. In addition, women and girls living some distance from their work must pay *$1* a month to the wheelbarrow coolie. From six to fourteen girls, according to size, bargain with a barrow coolie for transportation twice a day. The loaded wheelbarrows arriving one after the other before the gates of the factories are resplendent on sunny days with the bright colors of the garments of the girls, and in wet weather they are roofed over with brown fish-skin umbrellas and edged with a row of clumsy water-buffalo overshoes.

The older women contribute their earnings to the family funds, or perhaps, while their husbands gamble in the tea-houses, actually support the family. A certain man that left his wife and married a second, who was earning more money than he, is a not unfamiliar type of husband. Relying upon his second wife's wage, he himself worked but part time and refused to contribute anything to the support of his first wife. She was then forced to gain her own living in a factory. When he learned that she, too, was making money, he gave up work entirely and is now living comfortably on the joint income of his two wives.

The younger women contribute something toward the family expenses and spend the rest on their own adornment, unless they are saving for a trousseau, education, or a visit to some other city. It is not uncommon to see a factory girl dressed in light silk from collar to slippers come out of a home in which sits a woman with shrunken cheeks and a ragged child or two. Girls rooming with relatives and friends have more expenses, naturally, than those living at home. They pay about $4.50 a month for a room and from $3 to $6 for food. The average young woman spends between $15 and $25 a year for dress, except when she extravagantly invests as much as $5 or $6 at once in a woolen shawl. Unlike the older women and girls, most of whom make their own clothes and shoes, the younger girl has in many cases never had time to learn. She wears gay garments; for, while unmarried, she does not have to don the regulation work-dress of blue and black coat and trousers, usually of nankeen; but is free to indulge her love for color. It is pleasant among dark walls and machinery to come upon an operative in purple shoes, pink stockings, light blue trousers and a white, lavender or pale green coat. Groups of girls returning to the factory at noon flutter and waver about the streets like bright butterflies.

Many of the foreign factories close down over Sunday, and their operatives make up the aristocracy of labor. For the girls this holiday means an opportunity to sleep longer, wash their clothes, shampoo their hair, bathe and dress in their best. It has the possibility of a tea-party, a shopping-tour into the city or a moving-picture. The girls have decided preferences among stars. Charlie Chaplin and Harold Lloyd and anyone who takes the lead in a detective story are their favorites. Romances do not appeal; they " belong all same fashion."

For the older women Sunday very likely means no more than a chance to work all day at home. For them there are, indeed, but few compensations in factory life. Many of them are bearing children but dare not give up their work until they are forced to, because if they do, the family income stops. As soon as possible, usually within two weeks after the birth of the baby, the mother returns to claim her old tool. Some factories allow the mother to bring her baby with her and keep it in a low tub beside her or under her machine. More and more of the factories are refusing this privilege now, and the moths must turn the babies over to wet-nurses during their absence.

Something more powerful than birth-control societies or even than reverence for one's ancestors is tending to check repopulation. And this something, it appears, may be industry. Women earning their own wage are not disposed to give up their freedom and retire for some weeks or possibly months into the home to care for a baby and sew or make boxes on the side for eight or ten coppers a day, instead of the thirtycents they could get in the factory. The men, in whom ancestor-worship is inborn, and who feel that, unless they maintain their responsibilities in worship, they will suffer misfortune and agony in the next world, see foreigners, with but one wife, no children and no ties with the past, prosperous and happy. They see the Chinese returned students and superintendents who have been educated and trained in the West marry but one wife and live in safety whether a son is born or not. Except in so far as lack of funds and time prevents, the adult workers of this generation carry on the necessary family rites and observe the old customs, but they have neither time nor energy to train their children, who often grow to maturity without ever having seen their ancestral home. It is reasonable to suppose, therefore, that with the generations the sense of responsibility to the past — of the duty of reverence incumbent upon sons in a household — will decrease among the industrial workers.

Though the effect of industry on marriage and the position of women is more noticeable and at present more profound than on the birth rate, it is true that in some places there is little change. It was customary among the poorer families for a daughter to be betrothed while very young and sent to the home of her prospective husband, there to live . and work as his mother's servant. The bride still goes to the home of the bridegroom some months or even years before the marriage ceremony, but now she can go as easily from there to the factory as from her own home, and the ceremony can take place with less expense. Had the bridegroom waited until later for his bride, he would have had to pay a greater price in proportion to her increased earning-power. And whether she remains in the home of her father-in-law or returns with her husband to work in the factory, she is none the less subject, in some dis-tricis, at least, to her mother-in-law.

Social customs are growing flexible, however, among the workers. Though once the bride went alone to the house of her husband and it was unknown for the mother to accompany the daughter, there are now many homes in which the bride's mother is living in complete harmony with the husband's family. It would have been even more unusual for the bridegroom to enter the bride's family. Yet now in factory districts there are several young husbands living in the house of the wife's mother because the wife prefers that arrangement or it is cheaper, more convenient. Also, it is no longer a matter of inviolable precedent to live with the husband's father.

In the older industrial districts, and particularly in (Shanghai, every relationship between men and women has been affected by factory life. Each group is more independent of the other and independent of parental authority. Behind insurrection lies the fact that marriage long has been arranged on the basis of family expediency without any regard for the preferences of the bridal pair. But Eastern young men and women are no less human than those of the West and they usually make their declarations of independence in order to replace the one whom they do not want with the one whom they do.

As an outcome of this rebellion against the old marriage customs, elopements are numerous. Boys and girls thrown together in factory workrooms will elope in order to free themselves of their betrothals or through fear that their parents will not agree to their marriage. Such is often the case, and they return to the factory after a few days, sadder, if not wiser. Being disowned by their parents is a privation small enough in point of material wealth, but great in the loss of " face " and in isolation from a family group.

China proper is inclined to look upon Shanghai as a hotbed of iniquity and scandalous living. " Marriage, in Shanghai," said one official, " is a thing of pleasure and disgust. Divorce is common. So are elopements, broken contracts, broken marriages and loose morals." To some degree this is as true of the working classes as of the highest official and business groups. The new wife feels no obligation to merge herself in her husband's family nor to subordinate her interests to those of the other members. If they do not like her or she does not like them, she knows that she is capable of earning her own living without them.

Girls now in the factories are in no hurry to marry; nor are they willing to be led blindly into marriage. They feel that, if they are capable of earning their own living, they are capable of choosing their own husbands. An industrial district in Shanghai was recently rocked to its foundations by the refusal of a factory girl to marry the farmer to whom her parents had betrothed her as a child. On her wage she could buy herself better clothes than he or any other man of her class could give her. She was free from domination by a mother-in-law. She could go about at will in a city of lights and exciting activities. Both her family and the bridegroom's lost " face," as did also the priests and the village men who were brought in to convince her of her duty. But although Chinese women for centuries have obeyed what seemed an unbreakable law in regard to betrothal, no way was found to compel this one little factory girl to marry a man she did not want.

And now the girls in the better-class factories, intoxicated with freedom and confident of their own judgment, are declining to consider marriage at all. One factory has a small club of girls who have sworn to refuse all comers. In another, the head forewoman is unmarried and twenty-eight. She is called " Aunt" by both men and women and looked up to with admiration. A few years ago she would have been an object of derision, and even today she would be so in interior China, and, if alive at all, would be reckoned among the family liabilities.

The same condition prevails among the men. Young men between twenty and twenty-five, who formerly would have been married several years by this time, are now enjoying the independence of bachelor life. They can satisfy the deep desire of every Chinese to dress well. They can attend theaters, feasts, gambling-parties. Best of all, free from home responsibilities and ceremonies, they can devote their excess energies to advancing in their work.

Westerners can scarcely appreciate the radicalism of the method employed by these industrial rebels for making their own marriage arrangements. The case of Tong, an office clerk in an American factory, will serve to explain this statement. Tong became very much interested in a young forewoman. He came of a good family and had had two years in a Chinese university. She, although uneducated and of a lower-class family, was nevertheless capable and attractive. He broke all precedent and asked her personally to marry him. Her reply, that she was not the one to determine such matters but would abide by her father's decision, would seem ali that could be wished from a well-brought-up Chinese daughter. Yet Tong knew, and she knew that he knew, that, if her reply had not meant an enthusiastic yes, she would have answered very differently.

The most promising result of marriages between men and women who have come together through their work in the factories is the raising of the position of women in the household. Since the wife can earn in many instances as much as the husband and since she, too, contributes to the up-keep of their home, they are more nearly equals and are more companionable. They go to the theater together and ask friends in to small feasts. Instead of isolating herself when her husband's friends enter the house, the wife shares equally with her husband the responsibility and pleasure of entertaining them.

But this freer and happier domesticity is the gift of factory life to only a fraction of the hundreds of thousands employed in industry. In the various factories existence is bad enough for the women, but in the cotton-mills and silk-filatures it is utter misery. They are on their feet twelve, fourteen and, once every other week, as long as sixteen hours a day. Their hair and clothes are covered with drifting lint. They eat their rice as they stand beside the machines or sit on them. The air is stale, and the light from the windows at the sides is insufficient to reach the center of the vast workrooms. In the silk-filatures the women can sit at their machines, but are never allowed to have the windows opened even on the warmest days, because the fresh air affects the quality of the silk as it comes from the cocoons. The women sit all day with their hair moist and the perspiration running down beneath their coats. Or they may even be driven to removing their coats and catching just a strip of cloth across their breasts. Since even in the warmest days of summer, the Chinese woman never loosens her collar, conditions that force her to remove her coat while in the same room with men are wretched indeed.

In one mill in Wusih, women are able to work only three months at a time. The average factory life of such women is little more than two years. In another mill there are over a hundred women on call to take the places of those who have to drop out during the day. One mill provides extra workers to relieve the regular workers for an hour, but, since the women are on piece-work rates, they prefer to work until forced to give up. Most of the mills have arrangements with hospitals to care for injuries to operatives, but they will not do anything for the women who suffer from chilblains. To this complaint workers in the filatures are specially subject; for they have their hands in and out of scalding water all day, and then they go from the moist workrooms to their unheated homes.

Industry has brought to China and is creating there evils that fall heavily on the women. But it has also set at work during the past few years influences that mean more for the freedom and progress of working women than have all the generations of missionaries. The daughters of the poor have been sold into marriage as into slavery. But the knowledge that they can do more than cook and sew, that in man's own field they can earn in some cases as much as men, is giving them confidence. They are less afraid to assert their rights when imposed upon. The terror of the older woman that a protest will rob her of her chance to earn means nothing to the worker of the younger generation. She is sure of her ability. If she cannot stay in the knitting factory, mas *kee!* she can try an egg-packing factory.

During the past two years unions have been organized in the different industrial centers. Women have been permitted recently to become members of the cotton-mill, knitting-mill and several other unions. The women of the silk-filatures have their own union. In Canton there is a woman's union organized to protect the interests of working women in any industry. Women have taken part in several strikes during the past two years. But by many of the unions they are said to be a handicap. They are less reasonable than men. They go to more bitter extremes. On the other hand, they have not the resistance of the men. When they see their children hungry and cold, they forget their promises to stay away until the increase in wage and the decrease in hours are granted.

In August, 1922, however, several thousand woman workers in the silk-filatures went on strike independently as a protest against long hours, low wages, poor conditions. They lost, of course, but that fact is immaterial. On the heels of the strike, organizations representing nine hundred thousand woman workers, including those who took part in the silk-filature strike, appealed to the Governor of Kiangsu Province to reduce their hours of labor. Nominally, they said, they were to work eleven hours a day, but actually they worked fourteen. Under these conditions, especially in the summer, their health was seriously affected. One can hardly estimate in words the significance of these protests. The means used by the employers to break the strike show that they are fully aware of things to come. The women strikers in Chinese territorywere accused of infringing martial law and threatened with punishment under the military code. Strikers in the foreign settlement were brought into the Mixed Court and charged with " inciting workers to strike." There have been many strikes in Shanghai, but no such action has ever been taken toward the men.

The entrance of women into industry has been followed by the entrance of women into business and the professions. There are Chinese women doctors, teachers, bankers, advertisement-writers, journalists, secretaries, proof-readers, telephone-operators. In organizing to better themselves, they have realized the needs of the factory woman. The business woman's club of Shanghai, for example, provides supervisors for factory playgrounds and teachers for groups of workers who will organize. Chinese women are training in both Shanghai and America to enter the factories as what might be called " deans of women " to look after the conditions and influences under which workers labor.

According to Mr. C. C. Nieh, president of the Chinese Chamber of Commerce in Shanghai, Chinese women are feeling the effect of the feminist movement in the West. Whether or not this be true, woman's clubs are forming in the larger cities. Women are walking composedly about the Chinese stage, that exclusive domain of the Chinese man. Women are attending public dinners, theaters, shops, with or without their husbands. Women are traveling, swimming, playing tennis, dancing. Thousands are crowding into the schools and colleges of China; hundreds are sailing for Western schools. All this activity, though not making the life of the woman worker any more pleasant today, is rapidly increasing the numbers that will stand by her tomorrow, when the demand comes, as it must, for better conditions and freer opportunity.

Yet, whatever hope there may be for tomorrow, there is little chance today for advancement for Chinese women in industry. Ninety-nine per cent can neither read nor write sufficiently to keep the simplest records. They are influenced and surrounded by superstition. Although few workers can differentiate between Taoist and Buddhist priests, they usually have attended some temple three or four times a year. Now the long hours in the factory, the distance to the temple and the need of every copper for food and clothing are cutting these occasions down to one or none. Factory employees are too poor and too tired to go to the temples or even to honor Heaven on the first and fifteenth of the month with burning candles. The fact that their fortunes seem neither better nor worse as a result of this neglect does not encourage them to ardent efforts to visit the temples the next year.

Underneath all the organized faiths of China, lies animism, a belief in the existence of good and bad spirits. All classes are influenced greatly by this superstition, but the workers, because of ignorance and hardship, most of all. A fat volume sets forth the most necessary information concerning lucky and unlucky days, the procedure to be followed to obtain relief from the spirits and moral stories pointing out the necessity of complying with the wishes of these ghostly ones. Many families, whether or not they can read, possess this combined " Bible " and almanac; others refer to neighbors or to Taoist or Buddhist priests.

Industry makes ess impression on animism than on ancestor-worship, because, instead of merely cutting people off from the center of worship, it brings those from various districts with their various superstitions together and thus increases the circulation of new legends. The worker, whose life is many times but one hardship after another, readily believes that he is pursued by evil spirits and devotes much time and energy to outwitting them, especially in the interest of his children. Devils, it seems deem girls beneath their notice and confine their attention to boys. So the parents touch their sons' cheeks with red, fix earrings in their ears and call them by girls' names. Lucky coins and charms are placed about their necks and chains with bells about their ankles.

Nevertheless, the influence of industry is creeping like a slow tide into the shallows and bogs of superstition, and once in a while some incident marks its progress. It is supposed that a man falls ill because he has inadvertently misplaced his soul. If the soul can be found and brought back, he will recover. Relatives and friends of the sick one will take some of his clothing, a lantern and a large metal disk and visit all the places he has passed before his illness, beating on the disk and calling his name. At night they kindle small fires all along the road, to clear the road of devils and light the soul back to its home. Once when an operative in a factory fell ill with typhoid fever, the mother and sister appeared at the factory with the girl's coat, the lantern and the disk. They went up and down the aisle to her machine, round the machine and then down into another workroom where she had eaten her luncheon. It was significant that during the five years the factory had been operating, this was the first time such an event had occurred. Some of the workers accepted it as the proper procedure and hastened to advise and guide. Others were a little ashamed, others indifferent, others openly scornful.

It is also customary to believe that an eclipse of the moon is due to the ravages of a great dog which comes into the sky and swallows her. Since the moon is to the Chinese most precious and venerable, everyone flies to her rescue, beating pans and kettles, setting off firecrackers and shouting till at last the dog coughs her up and the noisy rescue is over. Priests pass around just before the eclipse and give warning. Because the morning after an all-night rescue party is hard on factory production, one manager took two or three of his trusty foremen aside and explained the passing of the shadow. The foremen thereupon prepared most of the factory personnel to watch the moon and the next morning reported to the manager that he was right.

8
CONFLICT AND CULTURE

THE CONFLICT BETWEEN NEEDED CHANGE AND OLD PATTERNS

While much is being said, and even attempted, in the way of mass education in China, the fact remains that without a radical revision of the present tools of knowledge — i.e., the present system of writing — such knowledge as is derived from books will remain a blank page to the great mass of the Chinese people, and universal literacy will remain at most a noble aspiration.

The difficulty is that of transcribing the Chinese language in a form which will be intelligible and at the same time can be learned with facility. Attempts have been made at Romanization, with little success, and the new phonetic script (the Djuyin) is also inadequate. The difficulty with both, of course, is the expression of the different tones of the Chinese language. When one writes " pu mai " it is of course quite unintelligible. It may be refusal to buy or a refusal to sell, just as " mai " may be an offer to sell or to buy. Different methods have been devised for the indication of the varying tones in Romanization, but even this has not achieved any widespread success, and does not seem likely to do so.

Writing as a Tool of Knowledge

Some system simpler than the old one is an absolute necessity, if there is ever to be universal education in the generally accepted sense of this word. Writing is in itself only a tool of knowledge — not knowledge in the larger sense. And so long as it requires years — as at present — to acquire the very tools of knowledge, so long will the great mass of the people lack learning, and. even the educated minority will be handicapped in their development by the time required in the gaining of these elementary things.

There will be general agreement that education involves the acquiring of knowledge gained through the experience of others, and that the written word is the best method of transmitting such knowledge.' Accordingly, mass education involves first of all instruction in reading — and with it of course in writing also.

The present system of writing in China makes literacy for the mass of the people an impossibility, so far as any time in the predictable future is concerned. A beginning has been made with the " thousand-character " system, but a person who has mastered these thousand characters is not literate in any real sense. One who is unable to read an ordinary newspaper can hardly be called literate, his reading being perforce confined to certain specially prepared literature.

To become literate in even an elementary way is a task of three years at least (taking of course the general run of students as a, basis). And that is only the very beginning of education. There is no likelihood in the present generation, therefore, of universal education in China. Yet universal education is a necessity, if the Chinese people are to take the place in the world to which their civilization and culture entitle them.

Present System Unsatisfactory

The fact must be faced that some other writing system than the present must be devised. The present characters (like the hieroglyphs of Egypt and Mesopotamia in the earlier days) are satisfactory for the education of a special class, but any attempt at universal education involves a simpler system. A phonetic system was worked out from the Egyptian hieroglyphs that was very probably the ancestor of the present Latin alphabet, but though the phonetic principle was introduced into Chinese in the compounds known as the hsing sheng, this was never carried out fully, and China still lags thousands of years behind Europe in this respect.

The scarcity of actual sounds in the Chinese language is to be regarded as largely responsible for this, and it seems likely that the continued use of hieroglyphs has further accentuated this scarcity by making the phonetic principle of minor importance. We find in the Cantonese language —probably the nearest to the early Chinese tongue —between 1,000 and 1,200 vocables. In the present *Pei-hwa* there are not more than half this number, and there is no doubt that the number has diminished in the past thousand years. If, as seems likely, the number of vocables has also diminished in Cantonese, it is probable that a few thousand years ago the Chinese language was quite capable of phonetic transcription without serious ambiguity. But we are now faced with the fact that such transcription (particularly of the Pei-hwa) is an impossibility.

Phonetics and Transcription

The only solution is to go directly to the root of the problem, and to make such modifications in the language itself as will make possible its clear expression in phonetic symbols. In other words, creating a new (or perhaps re-creating something akin to the old) form of Chinese. After all, we must remember that the present *Pei-hwa* is by no means a pure Chinese product. Many of its characteristics are due to modification by the Mongols and Manchus in Peking, e.g., the slurring of *tsi* and *ki* into the single sound *chi,* the loss of such endings as *t* and *k,* etc. The *Pei-hwa,* in fact, is probably the furthest removed from the original Chinese speech, and it is just the particular points which characterize the *Pei-hwa* which make phonetic transcription so difficult. Even today the Cantonese language, if its eight (or nine) tones are clearly indicated, is almost capable of phonetic transcription. The fact that the *Pei-hwa* contains but four tones is most striking, when we consider that the special intonation is one of the most characteristic features of the Chinese language.

So if we recognize that the making of education in China as universal as in most modern states is dependent upon the development of a method of writing as simple as in these other states, phonetic writing is an absolute essential, and there are only two ways in which this can be made successful. First, by taking some such form as Cantonese, making such modifications as are necessary to remove important ambiguities, writing it phonetically, and adopting it as the national tongue. Secondly, by creating a composite language (utilizing *Pei-hwa,* Cantonese, Shanghai dialect, and other forms) which can be written phonetically, and making this the national tongue.

Some of the Difficulties

The difficulty with the first method is that of instruction. It involves the utilization of all the tones of Cantonese, and the learning and teaching of four or five new tones is one of the most difficult things imaginable, particularly when carried out on a nation-wide scale. The advantage of the method would be that it would be based upon an already existing tongue, and there is also the sentimental advantage that it would probably be very much nearer to the true (i.e., the original) Chinese language than the present *Pei-hwa,* or than any artificial form that could be worked out.

Logically and practically, the second method is preferable. Not only would the number of tones not be increased, but it might be found quite practicable to eliminate them altogether, indicating differences in meaning by different vocables. If, for example, we permit the word " mai " to mean " buy " only, regardless of intonation and use the Shanghai form " ma " to mean " purchase," there would be no confusion.

Other common words could be treated in the same manner and a composite language created which would be easily learned by the mass of the Chinese people, based as it would be upon existing words in existing dialects, and involving no new principles such as the introduction of unfamiliar tones. Such a language would be readily acquired—in the time which it now takes to master the " thousand characters " — and in the working out of the language many problems of ambiguity could be definitely dealt with. The increase of the present number of vocables, of course, would be done by utilizing existing sounds to their fullest degree, for example *tsi* and *ki,* final *t* and *k,* perhaps final *p.* There are enough sounds in the Chinese language to render fully practicable a language which shall be expressible in phonetic symbols.

Until phonetic writing is made practicable, education in China will lag generations behind the rest of the world. The introduction of a clearly expressible system of language will make universal literacy in China not a far-off dream, but a goal which is possible of achievement in our own day and generation. It is a goal worth striving for.

ACCULTURATION : THE CONFLICT OF CULTURES

I recently had the curious experience of talking with a

young Japanese woman who was not only born in the United States, but was brought up in an American family, in an American college town, where she had almost no association with members of her own race. I found myself watching her expectantly for some slight accent, some gesture or intonation that would betray her racial origin. When I was not able, by the slightest expression, to detect the oriental mentality behind the oriental mask, I was still not able to escape the impression that I was listening to an American woman in a Japanese disguise.

A few months later I met this same young woman after she had returned from her first, and perhaps her last, visit to Japan. She was unusually reticent about her experiences, but explained that it was impossible for her to remain longer in Japan, although she had had every intention of doing so. She had found herself at a peculiar disadvantage there, because, though she looked like a Japanese, she was unable to speak the language; and besides, her dress, her language, everything about her, in fact, betrayed her American origin. The anomaly struck the Japanese public as something scandalous, almost uncanny. When she appeared on the streets, crowds followed her. They resented, perhaps even more at the time because of the recent passage of the Alien Land law, the appearance of a Japanese woman in the masquerade of an American lady.

Many of the early Japanese immigrants who came to California and settled with their families on the land, entertained rather romantic notions about America. They came with the deliberate purpose of casting in their lot with the American people, and rearing their children to be Americans. This was particularly true of the little Christian colony at Livingston, which is described elsewhere in this number. Mow, however, these Japanese pilgrims are restless and uncertain about their future. Many of them would like to return to Japan, but their children prefer to stay here.

Meanwhile, something extraordinary is taking place in these same children. They are growing up to be Americans, and, as such, are more or less disposed to accept the estimates of Japanese, and of all Orientals, which are current in the communities in which they live. Children acquire the prevailing attitudes in the community by a kind of moral infection, but even the adults are not immune, and there are moments when they are not wholly able to overcome that " sickening sense of inferiority " which overtakes most of us at times; moments when they could say, what members of other racial minorities have sometimes said: " I hate my race! I hate myself! " .

In this way the conflict between the Orient and the Occident, which presents itself in one of its aspects as external and international, assumes, in another aspect, the character of an internal and moral conflict. It becomes a conflict of loyalty; a struggle to knit together the strands of a divided self, to find a place to live, and preserve one's moral integrity in a world in which one can hardly hope for understanding or recognition. For the Oriental who is born in America and educated in our western schools is culturally an Occidental, even though he be racially an Oriental, and this is true to an extent that no one who has not investigated the matter disinterestedly and at first hand is ever likely to imagine.

ACCULTURATION : THE PROBLEM OF THE ALIEN

I was riding in a Pullman car last winter, returning home to Los Angeles from a visit in the East, when I struck up an acquaintance with the Negro porter. Seeing that I was not a white man, but a Japanese, he beckoned me to come into his inner sanctuary by the wash-room several times during the course of the long, monotonous journey; and there, as we sat secluded, the Negro whispered to me stories of his people.

This porter was an intelligent fellow, a college student

who was staying out of school that one year to make some money with which to continue his studies; and he seemed to know what he was talking about. Among the many things he told me, he dwelt at some length upon the difficulty which his people were experiencing in entering into suitable vocations. " I really don't know why I'm going to college," he confessed. " Outside of a few professions such as that of a physician or a teacher among our own people, there is no place in society for a college-educated Negro. The Negro is looked upon as a servant, and the white man will not recognize him as anything else. Why, I have several friends right on this railroad who are college graduates and now are working as Pullman porters; and in the eyes of the white man they are no different from any other Negro porter." That statement surprised me then, and I thought proudly to myself: " Thank goodness, we Japanese in America are not like the Negroes. We are not a servile people." I listened to the porter's story with a detached, condescending sympathy. But since then I have been thinking and observing, and recently, in my own experience, I have come across incidents which are forcing me reluctantly to wonder very seriously if the new generation of American-born Japanese on the Pacific coast is not facing the same problem as the Negroes in finding suitable vocations.

A few months ago I met an American-born Japanese fellow who had just been graduated with high honors in electrical engineering from a university of the Middle West. Every other member of his class had been offered a position before graduation, by electrical concerns near the university, and upon graduation they had stepped right into their professional field. But this one Japanese, simply because of his race, could not get a position. He had drifted to Los Angeles, still seeking work, and the last I heard of him was that he had finally secured a minor position in a little third-rate electrical shop in Honolulu, which offered practically no chance for advancement.

I know of another American-born Japanese who was graduated after specializing in foreign trade in the college of commerce of the foremost university on the Pacific coast. But no American firm would employ him as long as white applicants were available, although they might not be quite so capable as he, and no Japanese firm in America was doing enough business to need a specialist in foreign trade, so for months this man was without work. Finally, the manager of the San Francisco branch offices of the T.K.K. Steamship Lines took pity on him and gave him a position as a clerk in his office, at seventy dollars a month. Cases like these could be multiplied indefinitely.

The minor positions which these college graduates finally secured would not be so bad if there were some chance for advancement, for young graduates must all start at the bottom of the ladder. But there is very little chance to rise, for the Americans make no distinction between the second generation Japanese and the older Japanese, and we are all treated equally badly. It is impossible, at least on the Pacific coast, to imagine a Japanese in any high position which would require Americans to work under him. If, in order to avoid troublesome contact with American workers, we man a whole industry from top to bottom with Japanese, as we have tried to do in some fields, such as farming, fishing, and in some cases the hotel and restaurant business, the cries of " yellow peril " and " peaceful penetration " are immediately raised, and august state legislators feel it their duty to safeguard the commonwealth by taking drastic steps to oust us from our business by legislative measures. Or if we limit ourselves to businesses which cater only to the Japanese community, we are accused of being unassimilable and clannish, an undesirable element in American society. But however that may be, the Japanese community here in America is too small to support many businesses or professions by itself.

Our community is not self-sufficient. We can't stand off and live our own lives. We've got to find a place in American society in order to survive. And yet, no matter what our qualifications may be, evidently the only place where we are wanted is in positions that no American would care to fill — menial positions as house-servants, gardeners, vegetable peddlers, continually " yes, ma'am "-ing.

So, many of my friends are giving up the fight. "Why get an education? " they say. " Why try to do anything at all? Probably we weremeant to be just a servile class. We can't help it, so let's make the best of a bad bargain." These constitute the new shiftless, pleasure-seeking second-generation element in the heretofore industrious, thrifty Japanese community. The nicer individuals who accept this defeatist philosophy are a little more subtle. Instead of trying to drown out their unhappiness with mere pleasure-seeking, they turn to the church and religion to afford them comfort and relief from their economic and social misery, and they hold a cheaply optimistic, goody-goody idea that if they stay in their place, work hard and please the Americans and remain happy in the position where God has placed them, surely the Christian Americans, out of the generosity of their hearts, will throw out to them a few more crumbs to ease their condition. Personally, I see no use in the cheap optimism of that type of religion which would deaden the ambitions and aspirations of those who suffer from social injustice, so as to make them contented with their lot.

If it is so hard for us to get into suitable vocations here, why don't we go back to Japan? we are frequently asked. Only a few days ago I was walking across the Quad on our campus with an American classmate, and he turned around to me and said: " Gee! you fellows are lucky! Look at the great advantage you American-educated fellows have over the rest of your people when you go back to the old country."

I suppose his attitude reflects that of most Americans. " Well," I should like to ask, " what do you mean by going *back* to our old country? We've never been there in the first place." Most of us were born here, and we know no other country. This is " our old country " right here. As to having advantages over the people in Japan, we have the wonderful advantage of being quite unable to speak their language or read their papers, of being totally ignorant of their customs, history, or traditions, of holding different ideals, of thinking in different ways. Yes, we have as much advantage over the people in Japan as a deaf mute has over a man in possession of all his faculties. An American would have an infinitely easier time in Japan than we would, for they would excuse a foreigner if he made mistakes, but we, with our Japanese names and faces, would have to conform to their rigid standards or else be " queer." As for advantage in education, with some of the universities over there like Imperial, Waseda, and others ranking with the leading universities of the world, what chance have we products of the American rah-rah system against their mature scholars? The trouble with us is that we have been too thoroughly Americanized. We have attended American schools, we speak English exclusively, we know practically nothing of Japan except what an average American knows; our ideals, customs, mode of thinking, our whole psychology is American. Although physically we are Japanese, culturally we are Americans. We simply are not capable of fitting into Japanese society, so we are destined to remain here.

Yet, placed as we are between the devil and the deep sea, some of us are willing even to take the chance of going to Japan to seek our fortunes there. One of my friends, a chemist by training, unable to find a position here as such, is soon to leave to try his luck in adapting himself to Japan. Another, a girl about to be graduated from the university after specializing in secretarial training, said to me: " After I graduate, what can I do here? No American firm will employ me. All I can hope to become here is a bookkeeper in one of the little Japanese dry goods stores in the Little Tokyo section of Los Angeles, or else be a stenographer to the Japanese lawyer here." So now she is planning to go to Japan, where she has already been promised a position in a large shipping concern.

"If I should get married over there," she confided to me jokingly, " there is nothing to prevent me from getting a prime minister for my husband; but if I remain here, I can marry only a gardener, or a cook, or at best a small merchant; or, if very fortunate, a dentist or a doctor." Among my friends, I know two other American-born Japanese girls who are soon going to Japan, both as teachers of English in the schools there. Some of the most valuable of the American-born Japanese are going to Japan and are being lost to America. No doubt they can do their work properly over there, but I am wondering what satisfaction they will get, living alone among strangers in a land that is entirely foreign to them, fighting against a whole social system into which they do not fit.

But others of our group intend to stay here and see the thing through. We don't intend to succumb to our environment. We believe that our duty is to stay here and make a distinctive contribution to American life just as other national groups have contributed to American life in the past. But in order to make this contribution we must be given the opportunity to develop ourselves normally. Our immediate outlook is of course very dark. But our policy is to get the best education we can, to hold to the highest ideals we know, and to keep ever before us the vision of what we might accomplish, even though for a while we cannot find vocations befitting our abilities. Then we shall be so dissatisfied with existing conditions that we shall be working continuously to change them. Only by such continuous hammering away will any change come about. Of course it is going to be hard on the individual who will have to plug away at an inferior position when he is really capable of something better. But this seems to be the Only course which will bring any ultimate improvement. And to the credit of the American-born Japanese, many of them are following this policy, and a few of them are beginning to find their proper places in society.

For myself, I am frankly puzzled. I see some of my friends practically admitting defeat and settling down to a life of docile servitude. I see others of my friends so impatient that they are willing to take the desperate gamble of trying to adapt themselves to life in Japan. And Isee still others buckling down to the long and difficult task of trying to change conditions. None of the three ways seems very inviting to me, but I suppose that my sympathy lies with the last group.

CULTURAL INERTIA : RESISTANCE TO INVENTIONS

The commonplace use of various agents for the relief of pain in surgical operations is taken for granted at the present time, and the most important discovery of American medicine in the last century is in danger of being forgotten. Surgery without anesthetics is too horrible to contemplate, yet not until 1846 was there a practical means of controlling pain. But at the time there were four principal claimants of the title of discovery, all of them Americans and all responsible for so much bickering and blustering that the true magnitude of the discovery was clouded and is today forgotten, while all the mechanical products of American ingenuity are still praised as the greatest contribution to humanity.

The slightest operation in pre-anesthetic times was deservedly viewed with horror and repugnance. John Hunter, the famous English surgeon, spoke of operations as " humiliating examples of the inexpertness of science," and of surgeons as " no better than armed savages."

The surgeons themselves looked upon operative surgery as the lowest and poorest branch of the profession, and care and finesse were forgotten in the attempt to minimize the patient's suffering.

Still there were some who became hardened to the profession, and in 1784 one James Moore, a member of the Surgeons Company of London, published a pamphlet descriptive of a ?" Method of Preventing or Diminishing Pain in Several Operations of Surgery." There was no remarkable advance described in his paper, but the introductory paragraphs are so accurate a comment on early medicine that they are well worth repeating.

He says:

If any of the professions were in a particular manner to be distinguished by the name of humane, we might naturally expect — it would be that whose particular object it is to relieve the sufferings of humanity. And, if a greater degree of compassion and sympathy were looked for among any one class than any other, we should expect to find it in the breasts of those who pass their lives in the duties of so benevolent a profession as physicians. Physicians have been accused of a want of feeling for the distresses of human nature and surgeons of actual cruelty.

The lack of consideration for those in pain was not, however, due to lack of interest but to a lack of agents to control pain. From the earliest period of medical history there are stories of various schemes to control pain. Opium, laudanum, alcohol and such drugs were tried and found wanting. After Mesmer spread his mysterious doctrines, hypnotism was used with considerable success. But there was nothing that was easily and universally applicable to all cases, and the general public had good reason for avoiding the early hospitals.

It remained for a young American citizen to perfect a process that is still in use with very little change. The natural expectation would be that he would be rewarded for his work, but, to the contrary, never was a man more abused and never were more absurd attempts made to discredit a product of patient and careful experimentation. Even today there are some groups that wish to deny any honor to him, although for the great part this is due to local sectional jealousy and not from the violent personal hatred that was so evident at the time.

There were several individuals, all of whom were possessed of suffi-cient experimental information to obtain credit for the discovery, but either through fear, carelessness or lack of proper appreciation of its value they all withheld their knowledge till after Dr. W. T. G. Morton had braved the unknown and demonstrated the possibilities of ether. A careful study of the evidence can not help but convince the unprejudiced observer that Morton was alone responsible for the introduction of ether into use as an anesthetic, although Dr. Horace Wells, of Hartford, Connecticut, and Dr. Charles Jackson, of Boston, were working along the same lines and Morton very probably worked with them to some extent. Dr. Crawford Long, of Atlanta, Georgia, had used ether prior to Morton, but as I shall show later did not fully appreciate the importance of the material.

Morton was born in Charlton, Worcester County, Massachusetts, on August 19, 1819. His education was slightly better than the ordinary and from earliest childhood he tried to fit himself to become a physician. From various reasons, principally lack of funds, he was unable to achieve his ambition and we find him in early manhood shifting back and forth from one job to another. A disastrous business venture caused him to become dissatisfied with a commercial career, and he decided to take up some profession, even though it could not be the very one he wanted. The dental profession had just broken away from medicine and founded its own schools, and as this had some resemblance to his earlier desire, young Morton decided to take up dentistry.

At this period, dentistry left much to be desirec. Dr. Chapin A. Harris, a founder of the first dental school, said in 1840: " The profession is crowded with individuals, ignorant alike of its theory and practice, and hence its character has suffered in public estimation — the calling of the dentist has been resorted to by the ignorant and illiterate and, I am sorry to say, in too many instances by the unprincipled. . . ." This was none too severe an indictment, and it was onlythrough the efforts of such men as Harris and Morton that dentistry was to survive as a separate profession and eventually become recognized as one of public necessity.

The Baltimore College of Dental Surgery was founded in 1840, and Morton was one of the early students. While there he met Horace Wells and later they set up in partnership in Boston. As usual with such affairs there was not enough business for both and they separated, Wells going to Hartford and Morton staying in Boston.

At this time there were many lecturers touring the country who gave entertainments at the clubs and lyceums, where the natives of the smaller communities whiled away the winter hours. Among these was a Mr. G. Q. Colton, who came to Hartford and gave a demonstration and lecture on nitrous oxide, or " laughing gas," as it was popularly known. When the gas is administered in an impure state the characteristic symptoms of exhilaration are quite amusing to an audience and his lecture was very generally successful. Dr. Wells was very much interested and induced Colton to give a private demonstration on December 11, 1844. At this time Wells noticed that the subject was immune to physical pain. This fact made him wonder whether or not he could use it for his purposes, so he voluntarily took the nitrous oxide and while under its influence he had a tooth removed by Dr. John M. Riggs. This is the first recorded instance of a surgical operation deliberately performed on an individual while under the influence of nitrous oxide. Wells experimented during the winter and used his own patients as subjects. Early in 1845 he went to Boston to give a demonstration before Dr. John Warren's class of medical students. Owing to poor equipment or haphazard administration he was totally unsuccessful, for the patient cried out, the students jeered and Wells returned to Hartford discouraged and discredited. His lack of experience alone prevented him from being successful, but the entire matter so weighed on his high-strung mind that he retired from practice, and after a short stay abroad he committed suicide. This tragic ending, together with Wells's pleasing personality, did much to bring trouble on Morton's head at a later date. Wells should have all the credit that is justly due him, but if the world had been compelled to wait for some development to come from his work, there would have been a much longer period of time before the process was entirely perfected. As a matter of fact nitrous oxide was practically abandoned until G. Q. Colton resurrected the method in 1862.

Morton had assisted Wells at this fiasco and they must have discussed the subject thoroughly, but outside of the fact that Wells tried and failed at a public demonstration, while Morton tried and succeeded, there is no reason to believe that one helped the other to any great extent. The inhalation of fumes in medical practice was no new feature; in fact, ether was used in extreme cases of consumption and had been used as a local refrigerant at various times. Wells and Morton were working along the same lines and it is no wonder that it is difficult to assign credit definitely to one or the other, for they were associates and students together during the entire period, up until Wells's public demonstration. Morton had begun to work along different lines, and he drew as much inspiration from other sources as he did from Wells.

After the break in partnership, Morton had prospered, in fact, work came in so rapidly that he was compelled to hire several assistants. He had made several improvements in dental technique, and he was one of the best known practitioners in the city. His craving for a medical education still remained unsatisfied, so that in 1844 he entered Harvard Medical School. Morton was required to select one man from among the medical men of the city as preceptor or guide, and he chose Dr. Charles T. Jackson, then acknowledged the foremost chemist of the city and the one man most likely to help Morton in his work. The latter had not completely hidden the fact that he hoped to find some agent capable of deadening pain and Jackson had suggested sulphuric ether as a local application over sensitive tissue and they had discussed the properties of several other drugs at various times. Jackson claimed later that he knew that sulphuric ether would produce stupefaction when inhaled, but he did not make any such assertion publicly prior to Morton's demonstration.

The few known facts concerning ether impressed Morton and he set himself to determine all the properties of the substance. He read what little he could find and experimented with ether on small animals and on himself. It was customary for those who knew a little about ether to inhale the fumes up to the point where dizziness and a slight degree of intoxication was produced. This "ether jag" was well known among medical students and chemists and was practiced more or less openly. Morton tried to carry the state beyond the intoxication stage and at one time made himself deathly ill by inhaling the fumes of ether and opium together. His attendance at the medical school must have been rather sketchy, for he was carrying on these experiments together with his dental practice at the same time.

On September 30, 1846, he administered the ether to

one Eben Frost for the extraction of a tooth. The next day the Boston *Evening Journal* published a news item concerning this event. Morton then felt that he must give a public demonstration, so he went to Dr. John Warren, professor of surgery at the medical school, and asked permission to appear before the surgical clinic at the Massachusetts General Hospital. Warren had known Morton for some time and had a good opinion of the latter's professional attainments, so he readily gave consent. In this matter Morton showed that he was willing to jeopardize his reputation by appearing before the same group that had condemned Wells.

At that time the Massachusetts General Hospital was the largest and best in the city of Boston, and in addition to its size and conveniencehad a surgical staff that was second to none in the country. The building was an impressive structure, standing as it did near the Charles River, where the stately Bulfinch dome and granite columns at the entrance gave an air of dignity and eminence that was well upheld by the standards of medical practice of the institution. It was especially noted for the neatness and cleanness of the interior, a matter that was as generally emphasized in the hospitals of that time as it is today.

The operating amphitheater was directly under the dome and presented a much different appearance than the tiled and aseptic rooms now in use. Around about the old room were large cases containing surgical instruments, while chairs and tables of curious and unusual contruction were scattered here and there about the pit. The many hooks, rings, pulleys and other restraining devices that were to be found on the walls all testified to the necessary brutality of surgery of the period. The profound learning of Boston medical society was shown by the presence of an Egyptian mummy whose lugubrious countenance must have been an ever-inspiring spectacle in this den of horrors. The surgeons themselves were accustomed to come directly from their offices in all the glory of whiskers, stove-pipe hats and frock coats, with their spare instruments in their pockets, for sterilization was as yet unknown and patients still died of " bilious fevers " and " humours." There was generally a crowd of medical students on the benches that sloped up in tiers from the pit, and their appearance could not have been very inspiring, for the students of that age were notoriously unkempt.

Warren had set the date for October 16, 1846, and there was to be a representative gathering of the surgeons of the city. There had already been much angry discussion as to the possibility of Morton doing what he claimed, and there was a considerable group that did not like him personally, for his rather shy nature and the fact that he was only a dentist or at best merely a medical student was not entirely in his favor.

There was great difficulty in getting an inhaler suitable for the occasion. As there was no precedent for this work, Morton was accustomed to administer the ether from a bottle with a long snout that was inserted in the patient's mouth and on which he sucked rather than by the administration of the ether with a mask over the mouth and nostrils as is done today. The instrument maker was not able to devise an appliance that entirely satisfied Morton and at last he took a hand and made something up to his own specifications. Warren was kept waiting beyond the time agreed upon, and he had about decided that Morton had failed him, so that he turned to his colleagues and said, " As Dr. Morton has not arrived, I presume he is otherwise engaged." Just then Morton came. The patient was willing to have anything done to alleviate the pain and with few preliminaries the administration began. The spectators rather expected a repetition of the Wells fiasco, but nothing unusual happened and the patient soon lapsed into a deep slumber. Morton turned to Warren and said," Your patient is ready, sir "; and the operation was begun while an astounded silence fell on the room. Accustomed as the surgeons were to the struggles and torture of their patients, this seemed like black magic. Warren finished and broke the silence with, '? Gentlemen, this is no humbug." Dr. Bigelow chimed in with, " I have seen something today that will go round the world." There should have been a prayer of thanksgiving offered up in the old Puritan town on that occasion if ever.

The news spread rapidly and Morton was called upon to administer the ether for many cases. There were many references to the discovery in the Boston and New York papers, at first quite complimentary, but soon there was criticism and doubt as to the merit of the preparation. Morton had added some aromatic oils to the sulphuric ether to disguise the odor, but he had told the surgeons at the hospital that the active agent was none other than the ether. There was nothing essentially wrong in Morton's conduct in this regard, for he had assumed an immense amount of risk in his experimental and practical use of the agent, and the unpleasant results that followed when the application was in unskilled hands only emphasized this point.

Unexpected opposition came from some of the clergy, based on the assumption that pain was the direct consequence of original sin and therefore must be endured. Morton was threatened with prosecution and there was general condemnation of this terrible drug that set aside the laws of God and man. Dire pictures were painted of the use of this drug by criminals and all the hysterical fire of misguided religious zeal was brought to bear upon the matter.

One clergyman wrote of ether as " a decoy in the hands of Satan, apparently offering itself to bless Woman, but in the end it will harden society and rob God of the deep earnest cries that rise in time of trouble for help." Such stupidity seems incredible, but there were to be even more serious attempts to discredit Morton. No scurrility was too harsh to be applied to him, and the half truths and slighting comment often came from his neighbors and professional associates, the ones who were the first to be freed from that intolerable agony of pain that had so long burdened the human race.

Following the custom of the time, Morton patented his discovery. There is no doubt but that he hoped to profit by his effort, and in any other branch of endeavor there would have been no objection. However, there has always been considerable feeling among the medical and dental practitioners that humanity has need of every process for the alleviation of suffering without let or hindrance, so that rights and patents held by any one practitioner are foreign to the spirit of medical justice. Be that as it may, Morton gave his formula freely to the Massachusetts General Hospital without charge and only intended to profit by the sale of the preparation, called " Letheon." But everyoneknew that he was using ether and there was no particular need of buying a patented preparation when the pure ether could be obtained from a chemist.

It is interesting to note that the physician-author, Oliver Wendell Holmes, in a personal letter to Morton suggested the use of a new term " anesthesia " to describe the state produced by the application of the drug. Dr. Holmes continued as a friend and supporter, and it was only through the help of such men as Holmes, Warren and Bigelow that Morton was able to weather the storm that was about to break.

The opposition grew stronger within the first few months of the new year (1847), and the storm of protest and recrimination aimed at Morton fouled his fame and even today is responsible for the lack of appreciation of his work. The most abominable blow came from the members of his own profession in the form of a manifesto, published in the Boston *Daily Advertiser* and signed by Dr. J. J. Flagg and most of the leading dentists of Boston, making a formal protest against the use of ether and predicting all sorts of dire calamities from its use. This was to confront Morton at every turn and be used to discredit him when he went to other communities.

Cheap cynicism and irony were lavished upon the discovery by jealous medical men from less enlightened areas as follows:

Professor A. Westcott, of Baltimore, remarked that if Morton's sucking bottle would perform all the marvels accredited to it, the proper place for its use would be for squalling infants in the nursery; R. M. Huston, M.D., Philadelphia, "Quackery"; Wm. C. Roberts, M.D., New York City, " Humbug and a patented nostrum."

The editors of a New Orleans medical journal could not understand why the surgeons of Boston were captivated by such an invention, when mesmerism had accomplished a thousand times greater wonders.

It seemed as if the entire medical profession, outside of a few men in Boston, felt personally insulted that they had not been taken into confidence regarding this invention.

The efforts to discredit Morton are too loathsome to repeat. He was persecuted unmercifully, his dental practice broken up, his personal morals viciously attacked and every possible effort made to alienate any affection that his friends might have for him. The attacks were carried into his own home and he and his wife suffered endless humiliation. There was no limit to which his enemies would not go, and at times it was actually dangerous for him to appear in public. When he went to a small town near Boston to escape his persecutors, he was burned in effigy on the streets. Such humiliation is seldom the lot of him who has benefited mankind with one of the truly great gifts.

Dr. Jackson, his old preceptor, had been included with

Morton when the patent was taken out. The attorney advised that this be done, for Jackson had prior knowledge of the work and that might have been sufficient to bring the originality of the discovery into question. Jackson had refused to be included at first, saying that he might lose his professional standing by taking out a patent on a secret preparation. This objection he finally withdrew, and when the patent was issued Jackson was a co-patentee. Later Jackson was to claim the entire credit for the discovery in a letter to the French Academy of Sciences, and the final result was an extremely virulent quarrel between Morton and Jackson. The most that can be said of Jackson's claim is that more credence could be given to it if there were any record of his making a public statement concerning the properties of ether, prior to Morton's demonstration. If Jackson did know all about the material and its uses, as he very probably did, he was perfectly willing that Morton assume all the risk and responsibility for manslaughter that attached to the administration of the drug.

An application was made to Congress for recognition of Morton's discovery and to obtain an appropriation worthy of the work. The lawmakers were so hectored and flustered by the claims and counterclaims of the partisans of Jackson and Wells that they were unable to come to a definite agreement; no credit was given to anyone and Morton retired, poorer and more discouraged than ever.

There was an additional claimant at this time, one Dr. Crawford Long, of Georgia. He had seen ether used for jags and sprees, had experimented with it on some patients and, it is said, used ether for anesthetic purposes four years prior to Morton's public demonstration. The evidence is quite obscure on this, but Long himself admitted in the *Southern Medical and Surgical Journal* of December, 1849, that he had not progressed far enough to be sure of his ground. Such action as he took after the public interest in Morton's work would seem to be simply an effort to steal Morton's glory. Long abandoned his experimentation and certainly had no appreciation of the possibilities of the drug. He was simply one of the many others who had the chance to bring the hidden facts to light but was incapable of doing so. Sir Humphry Davy had written of nitrous oxide in 1800, that it was capable of producing stupefaction and insessibility to pain. The materials for all the discoveries that have blessed mankind have stood ready at hand since the beginning of time, but only those who are able to recognize and put the unknown to use should have credit as discoverers.

Wells and Long both deserved better fortune. Jackson has not a glimmer of justification in his claim, Morton succeeded where the others failed but reaped a whirlwind of abuse that was the most humiliating ever visited on a great pioneer.

The shoddy methods used to discredit Morton were entirely unjustified. The only considerable honor that he received in his lifetime was a gold medal from the French Academy of Sciences and an honorary medical degree from an American university. There is everyreason why his name should rank with that of the great Americans, for to him must go the entire credit of risking his life and happiness in order that mankind be freed from pain.

The epitaph on his tombstone in Mount Auburn Cemetery at Cambridge best describes his lasting claim to fame:

Dr. W. T. G. Morton

Born August 19 1819.

Died July 15 1868.

Inventor and Revealor of Anaesthetic Inhalation.

Before Whom in all Times Surgery was Agony.

By Whom Pain in Surgery was Averted and Annuled.

Since Whom Science Has Control of Pain.

CULTURE CONSERVATISM IN A TRANSPLANTED CULTURE GROUP

Along the Volga, where Europe merges with Asia, many Germans have settled, in a district known as the Volga Colonies.

Although the Volga Germans were occupied almost exclusively with agriculture, a few industries flourished within the villages, such as the making of shoes and the weaving of textiles. These, however, were merely to satisfy the demands of the household and those of fellow villagers. There was no trade between villages and no commercial enterprise linked the economic life of the village with the larger world.

From both the Meadow Side and the Mountain Side members of the colony emigrated to America, but the peoples from the respective Sides remain distinct. An invisible river flows through the new environment, a transplanted ghost of the Volga. Wherever he goes the Meadow Side man takes the Meadow Side of life, thought, and associations, and the Mountain Side man, similarly, takes the Mountain Side. Between them and separating them flows the Volga. The Mountain Side people have settled principally in Washington and Oregon, while the Meadow Side is represented in Nebraska, South Dakota, and California, the colony in Fresno being the largest community. There are about six thousand in the city and environs and about ten thousand in the county. The more progressive Mountain Side people, as is notably true of the Oregon colonies, have branched out into every walk of life; the Meadow Side people, in contrast, live the self-centered life which characterized them when they dwelt on the east bank of the Volga. Thus among the thousands who have settled in and around Fresno there are no physicians, dentists, lawyers, teachers, business managers, artists, nor musicians. They still live on the eastern bank of the Volga.

The German-Russians in Fresno are a hard-working, God-fearing people, who attend faithfully to their own affairs and do not meddle in the affairs of others. Drunkenness has been confined to the younger men, to those who were being " Americanized," and it has been rare among them. Saloons were never tolerated in the colony — instead they built churches. The people are straightforward, honest, and dependable, though some individuals are exceptions to the rule. As a community, however, they still constitute a German-Russian colony dwelling on the Meadow Side. The segregation that characterized them in the old country clings to them tenaciously in the new. If a wall were built around the colony, except for a few Armenians, mainly older settlers, there would be included within it scarcely a family that does not belong to the Volga colony, and few families within the city that belong to the colony would be left without it. Physical segregation, although it does not of necessity involve anything more, makes strongly for mental segregation, and in this instance the two are nearly synonymous. The area of the physical life is the area of the mental life; they have the same center and the same periphery. A common outlook overtops the varied individual perspective. Individuals do not enter the various pursuits, business or intellectual, which typify American life. American influence makes few breaches through the invisible wall.

The community is an atoll amid a sea of varied influences which surround but do not permeate. There is great confidence within the walls, and little poise and confidence without. The women still wear the shawl, instead of bonnet or hat, and are not to be distinguished in costume, speech, or appearance, from the women who still dwell along the Volga. When they go abroad into the town, a half dozen blocks away, they are as far away from home as when they left the Volga village and voyaged to America. They return to a Volga village, though that village of invisible walls is but ten minutes walk from the center of Fresno They look into our world, not out from it, and they see little more than the physical aspect of our life. Wherever they go they carry the Volga atmosphere with them; they do not live in the larger municipal world, and they know little about it.

The children are noisy and form gangs which make life miserable for those without as well as for those within the colony; for their confidence, at least within their immediate surroundings, knows no bounds. As soon, however, as they have left the corner of the city where they live, unless they go in large numbers, they are cowed and silenced; for they have left familiar associations and entered a strange world. Those who go to the high school, previously a small percentage, generally clique together, mingle little with other pupils, and few take an active or intelligent part in school affairs.

Near the German-Russian community is a playground frequented almost exclusively by them. To provide a more commodious playground,the city has contemplated the purchase of ground within two blocks of the present playground site, and beyond an irrigation " ditch " that runs along the present playground. But the people on " this side " of the ditch insist that their children shall not play on the " other side." Those who live on " this side " are the older settlers. Those who live on the " other side " do so, in the main, because there is no more dwelling space on " this side." Yet the former look down upon the others, who live, for them, beyond the Volga, on an inferior Meadow Side. When the writer first heard accounts of the antipathy between these two sections which are divided by an irrigation " ditch " that one can jump across, he was disposed to treat the matter as a bit of humorous exaggeration. Hearing it repeatedly however, and finally, being assured by the several ministers of the colony that such was the case, and receiving confirmation from numerous parents, he became convinced that a Volga was within as well as about the colony.

ISOLATION AND CULTURAL INERTIA

If the traveler to Hungary forsakes the usual haunts of tourists to wander into the more remote regions, he will discover, scattered over Hungary and even beyond the borders of the present state, a number of secluded sections where inhabitants, though speaking only the Hungarian language, yet differ in a marked manner from the Magyars around them in costume, dialect, and folk customs, while in each respect these groups show a remarkable similarity.

The problem of the origin of these remote groups is one that Hungarian ethnologists have struggled with for a long time. One thing is certain: they have absolutely no racial connection with the Germanic, Slavic, or other peoples with which the Hungarians have for many centuries been surrounded. They differ in certain respects from other Hungarians; yet in these very matters of costume, dialect, and folk customs the mass of the Magyar people shows far more decidedly the influence of neighboring peoples than does the population of these sections. One of the most notable features of their dialects is the absence of loan words which occur in great abundance in the speech of modern Hungary. I myself have had experience of the reality of dialectic differences during the course of my church work among Hungarians. My church has a constituency of about two thousand Hungarians from every section of the home country. So long as they speak in ordinary Hungarian they understand one another: how many tell me they cannot comprehend the speech of Gocsej or Sarkoz or Mezbkovesd! Szinnyei Josef's " Dictionary of Dialect," it may be noted, deals largely with the dialects of these isolated groups. Historical documents also confirm the racial differentiation of the groups.

The people of these sections usually claim with pride

that they alone are pure-blooded descendants of the ancestral Magyars and that they alone have preserved the ancient manners of the race; ethnologists formerly assented to this view, supposing that seclusion had preserved the ancestral speech and customs. During the last quarter of the nineteenth century and the first years of the twentieth a strong school of ethnologists has arisen in Hungary who hold that, though isolation doubtless favored the retention of ancient characteristics, close study of the case warrants no other conclusion than that these groups represent broken fragments of non-Magyar but related peoples. Where the seclusion was not sufficient, as in the case of the Kunok and Jaszok of the Alfold, the ancient racial characteristics disappeared and the tribes became completely merged in the Magyar population around them. There are, however, many other secluded regions as, for example, the valley of the Tarna in the county of Heves, whose inhabitants differ in no way from the ordinary Magyar people. The striking difference is observable only in those sections in which racial non-identity has been made more pronounced through long seclusion. One of the greatest difficulties in the study of Hungarian folklore is that the separate origin of much of the folklore of these detached regions has not yet been sufficiently recognized.

The Sarkoz

In the County of Tolna, between the mountain of Szekszard and the Danube, just across from Baja there lies a large level tract of exceedingly rich soil, the territory of the four villages of Ocseny, Decs, Sarpilis, and Alsonyek. The fertile land from which these villagers today reap abundant harvests was only a few decades ago a great swamp, from which the region derived its name of Sarkoz — Country of Mud. The hard struggle for existence in those days compelled the men of the villages to remain absent from home a great part of the year, during which time they either fished along the shallow water-courses of the marshland or else sought pasturage for their herds and flocks on the banks of the swamps. The women remained at home in the little villages, which were set as islands in the waste of swamp. Being left alone, they developed to an abnormal extent two of the tendencies found among the women of all these remote sections: thetendency, on the one hand, to find employment in the weaving and embroidering of beautiful folk costumes for themselves, and, on the other, to seek social life in clubs or guilds, each composed entirely of girls or women of a particular age.

Since the marshes have been drained and transformed from a worthless waste into land of almost incredible fertility, these people have suddenly found themselves the richest villagers in all Hungary; yet in spite of the changed conditions many of the old habits of life remain. As in the days when their husbands were occupied with fishing or herding, the women even now do little work other than the embroidering of their costumes. The only difference is that they are rich now and can afford to buy the most expensive materials. When Malonyay Dezso studied these villages in 1912, he found that the average girl's costume was worth 600—800 gold korona, i.e., $120—$160. When I visited these villages in 1925, I was told by many of the people that an average girl's costume costs now at least the equivalent of $300 and that every girl of well-to-do family possesses several costumes. In spite of the increased costliness of the materials used, the same folk motifs are embroidered on the silk of today as were worked into the homespun of two or three generations ago. When the village women deck themselves out in their finest array and assemble in front of the Reformed Church on Sunday morning — all the people of the Sarkoz are stanch Calvinists — the effect is almost indescribably beautiful. Malonyay compared it to a flower garden in which red and lilac colored flowers predominated against a green background: the silk dresses are very often green, and the embroidery shows almost every conceivable shade of red and mauve. Scattered among the bright colors are dresses of pure white; for white is the color of mourning in the Sarkoz, just as it is in Csokoly and the Ormansag. My own impression of the distinctive quality of the dresses worn in the Sarkoz is that, while the colors are bright, yet there is no such sharp contrast as in the color scheme of the dresses of Mezokovesd. There is here a softer and more harmonious blending.

Several customs are connected with the wearing of these costumes, many of them not limited to the Sarkoz but more or less prevalent through all these detached groups and even beyond them. Such a custom is that whereby a woman shows her family's wealth and importance by the number of petticoats she wears under her gloriously embroidered apron. Very often from thirteen to seventeen petticoats are worn, and the wearer is able only with great difficulty to enter the church door. The headdress of a woman indicates her condition, and the color of her clothes her age. There is a particular headdress — the *parta* — formerly with seven horns, to indicate the unmarried woman. Another headdress is substituted for this on the morning after her wedding. After the birth of her first child, her headdress is again changed. As the woman grows older she abandons more and more the gorgeous clothes of her girlhood. At forty she wears only white: at fifty only black. Yet of her coffin she is able once again to wear her bridal costume.

A peculiarity of several of the Sarkoz customs is the exclusion of men from the social group. Every girl becomes a member of one of the village bands, consisting of from fifteen to twenty girls under a recognized leader. Together they attend school; together they attend church on Sunday morning; together they take part in the peculiar dance in which no man is allowed to participate. After the birth of a child to a young married member of the band the somewhat mysterious custom of *csoroglo* is held: this is a sort of baptismal rite, wholly pagan in character and handed down from pre-Christian times. At the *csoroglo* only women may be present. After the rite some one is sent to announce to the father the birth of his child, just as in the old days when he would be far absent with his flock or fishing boat or be engaged in dressing the vineyard on the mountain side, and it is only after this announcement that the father is allowed to see his child. Another ancient custom is that of the *istenfa* — God's Tree — usually a rosemary shrub set out in the courtyard of each home. Before the woman of the house greets male visitors, she walks around the *istenfa* in order to secure protection from evil spirits.

Some of the old customs have now been dropped altogether. No longer do the youths chase the maidens through the vineyards and become betrothed to the one they are able to catch. Today marriage among these people is almost entirely a property consideration, worked out by the families of the prospective parties with a view to the enlarging of their estates. With a similar ambition before them the people have adopted the practice of birth control and limit the number of their offspring strictly to one child in the family. The worst effects of a rigorous birth control are perhaps more manifest in the Sarkoz and in the neighboring Reformed Church communities of Csokoly and the Ormansag than anywhere else in the world. The few children are usually very delicate; and most students of the situation predict that, though there are still between eight and nine thousand of these interesting people, in a few more decades they will be entirely extinct. There are not as many of them today as in 1720, when their ancestors were serfs on the domains of the Roman Catholic abbeys of Szekszard and Bataszek. Every traveler to these villages comments on the gloominess and desolation so discordant with the wealth of the villagers. Many houses are vacant: the families who lived in them have died out completely. Though the houses are large, the small family — grandparents, parents and the only child — find one or two rooms at the back sufficient for them to live in. All the spacious front rooms are unoccupied save by spare beds which are never used and by wardrobes in which are kept the gorgeous costumes of the women. This same desolation is to be observed in an even more marked degree among the less wealthy villagers of the Ormansag andCsokoly. As Mr. W. Stanley Lewis has suggested, the practice of birth control has been introduced through contact with Swabian settlers from South Germany. The pastor of Ocseny assured me it was due to the presence of South German officeholders who had been placed in the villages by the Austrian government after the collapse of the revolution of 1848.

A careful study of the people of Sarkoz along with an examination of the oldest documents relating to these villages shows almost conclusively that, in spite of their claim to be pure-blooded descendants of the ancestral Magyars, they are not Magyars at all but are descended from a tribe of Cumanians (Kunok) which joined the Magyars in the neighborhood of Kiev in those days before 896, when the Magyars under the leadership of Almos and Arpad were marching toward the Carpathians and their present home. These Cumanians were of an Ural-Altaic stock, closely related to the Magyars themselves. Unlike their kinsmen — Kunok and Jaszok— who entered Hungary in the thirteenth century and occupied extensive tracts in the Great Plain or Alfold between the Danube and the Tisza and east of the latter river, these Cumanians who entered at the time of the Invasion have retained their ancient customs. Those of the Alfold, on the contrary, have become completely merged with the Magyar people around them. Only the names of their towns and villages indicate their separate origin. Doubtless it was the long isolation caused by the marshlands of the Sarkoz which has preserved this distinctive type, while their kinsmen have completely lost their identity.

The interesting fact that these nine related but distinct groups have preserved ancestral customs and habits far better than the Magyars themselves is paralleled by the story of the Rechabites in the Book of Jeremiah. Doubtless the Rechabites were a nomadic tribe which had accompanied Israel at the conquest of Canaan. Centuries afterward when the prophet Jeremiah wished to find an example of the good customs of bygone days, he had to turn to these Rechabites who had remained in all things just like their fathers. So is it with these isolated races of Hungary. In speech, customs, and folk costumes they have remained like their fathers. Though not themselves descendants of the invading Magyars, they show us better than do the Magyars themselves how the ancestral Magyars lived, talked, and dressed.

9

Social Change and Social Problems

SURVIVALS AND SOCIAL CONSERVATISM

" The extraordinary ceremony of 'Anathema ' against M. Venizelos performed on Christmas Day (1916) by the ecclesiastical authorities of Athens at the instigation of the League of Reservists has had its uses — besides providing anthropologists with the most remarkable instance on record of the survival in Europe amid the forms of civilization of a magic ritual common to savages all over the world. The Metropolitan of Athens, as it was reported at the time, solemnly excommunicated a bull's head (which presumably represented the body of Venizelos), and cast the first stone; and then each member of the crowd assembled by King Constantine's hooligans cast a stone on the pile and uttered a curse against the man who had ' plotted against the King.' But King Constantine's appearance as a Hottentot witch-doctor had unexpected results, and only served to prove even in his own stronghold that all the terrorism of German autocracy could not quench the real devotion of the Greek people to M. Venizelos. From fuller accounts of the ceremony now received by the Anglo-Hellenic League it appears that during the night the cairn of stones so solemnly cursed and supposed to symbolize the ' casting out' of the ' traitor,' was covered with masses of flowers; and in the morning these bright garlands were seen to be attached to an inscription which read ' From the Venizelists of Athens.' "

This cursing and stoning of the great statesman and good patriot Venizelos, who has been banished from Athens by traitors, resembles the cursing and stoning of King David, when that great monarch was banished from Jerusalem by the treachery of his unnatural son Absalom, who had usurped the throne. As David and the procession of loyal men who followed their beloved king into exile were wending their way sadly down the steep road which descends from Jerusalem into the deep valley of the Jordan, a certain Benjamite named Shimei kept pace with them on the hillside above, and as he went he threw stones at the king and his escort and cursed, saying, " Begone, begone, thou man of Diood, and man of Belial! " This was more than one of the king's captains, a man of hot blood, could bear, and he asked David, " Why should this dead dog curse my lord the king? Let me go over, I pray thee, and take off his head." But the king received the curses and the stones with magnanimous patience, and rebuked the fiery Hotspur who would have washed out the insult on the spot with the caitiff's blood. He reminded his would-be champion that his own son, Absalom, was at that moment seeking his father's life, and " How much more," he asked, " may this Benjamite now do it? Let him alone, and let him curse; for the Lord hath bidden him. It may be that the Lord will look on the wrong done unto me, and that the Lord will requite me good for his cursing of me this day."

The king's trust in Providence was not misplaced. In a short time the traitor and usurper was defeated and slain, as he hung by the hair of his head in the forest which witnessed the discomfiture of the rebel army. The king came to his own again and returned in triumph to Jerusalem, the people flocking to welcome him at the ford over theJordan, which he had lately crossed in haste, a fugitive and an exile. And the first to meet him at the ford was the very man who had so lately cursed and stoned him. There stood Shimei, the Benjamite, waiting for him; and when the bearer who had carried the king through the water deposited his royal burden respectfully on the shore, the quondam railer and bully, now turned toady and lickspittle, fell on his face before the king and begged for mercy, saying, " Let not my lord impute iniquity unto me, neither do thou remember that which thy servant did perversely the day that my lord the king went out of Jerusalem, that the king should take it to his heart. For thy servant doth know that I have sinned: therefore, behold, I am come this day the first of all the house of Joseph to go down to meet my lord the king.". The same hot-headea soldier, who would have had Shimei's blood when he cursed and stoned the king, now earnestly requested to be allowed to take it when the fellow fawned and groveled before his Majesty. But again the king calmly checked the impetuosity of his too zealous adherent, saying that no blood should sully the happy day of the royal restoration. So saying, he turned to Shimei and gave him his life. " Thou shalt not die," he said, and confirmed the pardon with an oath.

The parallel is of happy augury for M. Venizelos. He, too, we believe, will return in honor and glory to his own in Athens, and he will doubtless complete the parallel by treating with the same magnanimous disdain the contemptible ecclesiastic who has cursed and stoned him.

The ritual by which the Metropolitan of Athens has disgraced his cloth and his Church, without inflicting the smallest harm on the object of his impotent wrath, is unquestionably of heathen origin, and, set off by the gorgeous habiliments of the officiating clergy, must have pre-spntprl the same sort of ludicrous medley which is sometimes displayed by the untutored savage, who struts and flaunts in a grotesque combination of native paint and foreign velvet. In Europe such mummeries only contribute to the public hilarity, and bring the Church which parades them into contempt.

The combination of stones and curses directed at a person who, for one reason or another, is out of reach seems to be not uncommon; ignorance and malignity apparently trust to one or other, if not both, of these missiles hitting their mark in some manner unexplained. The poet Propertius ungallantly invited all lovers to pelt with stones and curses the grave of a certain lady whose reputation, by a stretch of charity, might perhaps be described as dubious.

A writer on Syrian folklore has described " the customs with regard to casting curses or prayers with stones from the hand. All tourists to Jerusalem have seen Absalom's tomb, and the hole in the base of its pinnacle through which generations of Jews have conveyed thus their imprecations on an ungrateful and impious son. ... At Biskinta, on the Lebanon, is the tomb of a Druze who, tradition says, was buried alive to obtain merit in the next stage of his existence; for the Druzes believe in the transmigration of souls. Greek Orthodox Christians in the village — and they only — cast stones on this grave with muttered curses as they pass."

A traveler in Palestine has described how between Sidon and Tyre his Mohammedan companions discharged stones and curses, with equal force and volubility, at the grave of a celebrated robber who had been knocked on the head there some fifty years before, and who still continued to receive this double testimony to his character from passers-by, whose stones remained in a heap on the spot, while their curses had melted into thin air. After all a stone is perhaps a more effective missile to hurl at a man than a curse, unless, indeed, as Voltaire justly observed, the curse is accompanied with a sufficient dose of arsenic.

In view of the extraordinary persistence — we may almost say the indestructibility — of superstition, it seems likely that the remarkable rite of cursing recently directed against M. Venizelos has not been simply invented by his enemies, but that it is based on a tradition which has been handed down from antiquity, though I am not able to cite any exact parallel in ancient Greek literature. Euripides represents the adulterer and murderer, Aegisthus, flushed with wine, leaping on the grave of his victim and pelting it with stones, but he does not say that the villain reinforced with curses these expressions of his malignant hate. Perhaps a nearer resemblance to the modern ecclesiastical comedy, in which the Metropolitan of Athens took the principal part, may be found in the treatment which Plato in his Lows recommended should be meted out to the wretch who had murdered his father or mother, his brother or sister, his son or daughter. According to the philosopher, the criminal should be put to death and his body cast out naked at a crossroad outside of the city; then the magistrates should assemble, and each of them should cast a stone at the head of the corpse in order to purge the city from the pollution it had contracted by so heinous a crime. Here, again, the writer says nothing about any curses by which the throwing of stones may possibly have been accompanied. But the context proved that, in this part of his ideal legislation, Plato was less concerned with the punishment of the criminal than with the purification of the city, which was believed to have been defiled by his act; it may be, therefore, that imprecations formed no part of the ritual of purification contemplated by the philosopher. Whether that was so or not, we may surmise that, in prescribing this form of atonement for parricide, matricide, and similar aggravated cases of murder, Plato had his eye on certain expiatory rites which were either actually observed in his time or traditionally reported to have been observed by gods or men in former ages. For, with the growing conservatism of age, Plato in the Laws clipped those wings of his imagination which had borne him aloft in the *Republic* into the blue. In his later work he took a lower flight,and hovered much nearer to Greek earth and Greek usage than when he had surveyed the whole world from the empyrean heights of pure idealism. Now a ritual not unlike that which our philosopher prescribed in the case of parricide was said to have been observed at the trial of the great god Hermes for the murder of Argus. The gods, we are told, who sat in judgment on the divine prisoner at the bar, each cast a stone at him by way of purifying themselves from the pollution of his crime; hence the origin of those heaps of stones which, in ancient Greece, were to be seen by the wayside surmounted by images of Hermes, and to which every passer-by added a stone. Here, again, the casting of the stones is clearly a rite of purification rather than of commination, and it was probably not supposed to have been accompanied with curses.

The bull's head at which, in default of the head of M. Venizelos, the clerical and lay blackguards of Athens hurled their stones and curses, has its parallel in the sacrificial ritual of ancient Egypt. Herodotus tells us that the Egyptians used to sacrifice black bulls, and that when they had slaughtered the victim at the altar, they skinned the carcass, cut off the head, loaded it with curses, and sold it to any Greeks who might be resident in the town; but if there happened to be no Greek population in the place, the Egyptians carried the bull's head to the river and threw it into the water. The curses which they leveled at the bull's head consisted in an imprecation, that whatever evil was about to befall either the sacrificers themselves or the whole land of Egypt, might be diverted therefrom and concentrated on the head. Naturally, no native Egyptian would purchase a head laden with malisons so dreadful; but the Greek traders appear to have calculated, with great justice, that the cursed heads no doubt sold a good deal cheaper than common heads in the market, and were quite as good to eat; a shrewd Greek householder probably rather preferred to dine on a bull's head which had been blasted by the ecclesiastical thunder.

It will be observed that in this Egyptian rite the priests apparently confined themselves to loading the black bull's head with curses; they did not give point and weight to their maledictions by pelting it with stones. In short, in ancient Egyptian ritual we have found curses without stones, and in ancient Greek ritual stones without curses. The Metropolitan of Athens has combined both weapons, the material and the spiritual, in the assault, as futile as it was ridiculous, which he headed against the wisest and greatest of his countrymen. By the flowers, which next morning covered the shameful heap of stones, Greek patriotism converted the insult into a tribute of homage to the true leader of Greece.

THE LOSS OF TRAITS FOLLOWING SOCIAL CHANGE

A language is dying — intestate and without issue. At the height of its power and affluence, in the fullest possession of its faculties, with a literature, a theater, and a press of its own that would do honor to many a landed tongue, Yiddish in America is facing a slow but inevitable dissolution, dying — with no one to will all these accumulated riches to. In twenty years there will be no readers left for its great metropolitan dailies, no audiences for its numerous and now crowded theaters; and its contemporary literature — already readerless, and printed by the authors for mutual presentation — will be a closed set, a completed classic, like the four-and-twenty books of the Old Testament.

But it will be a painless end, a death in easy instalments, regulated by the 2 per cent ratio of the Immigration Act, that " cordon sanitaire " which our Nordically minded Congress has drawn around the Ghetto. On the East Side and its numerous suburbs in Manhattan, Brooklyn, and the Bronx the strange, angular characters on the store windows are growing scarcer and scarcer; and soon even the indispensable Kosher motto — the coat-of-arms of Jewish delicatessen and butcher shops — will be spelled in heathen English. Column by column the growing English sections of the Yiddish dailies will march across their pages in Occidental order from left to right, forcing the square right-to-left Oriental lettering backward; until at length the latter will be confined to A Yiddish Page for the Old, occupying the supplementary position at present held by An English Page for the Young.

On the Yiddish stage creative life is ebbing fast. There are more Yiddish theaters than ever, but nothing new has been written for them in years, except musical comedies differing very little from those on Broadway. The final stand of serious Yiddish drama, the Yiddish Art Theater, is planning in the future to alternate its Yiddish program with English; and an organization called the Anglo-Jewish Theater at the 66 Fifth Avenue Playhouse is producing Yiddish classics in English.

As for contemporary literature, it is something of academic or — to use an East Side paraphrase — of " cafe" interest only. . 'terary schools rise and fall in the cafe, but the street knows them not. The classics— Perez, Sholem Aleichem, Sholem Asch, Pinsky, and the 'est — have already been translated; and perhaps in the future a filial translated anthology — an "AND OTHERS" — will be complied and the matter considered closed.

In the Yiddish theatrical world there is very little fleep lost over the approaching demise. Actors are accustomed to having their art die with them; and as for the producers — theatrical undertakings as business enterprises are comparatively ephemeral things. Playhouses are built without lingual partiality. Their stages and box-offices can be adapted to English without any cost.

In the literary world there is more concern. The squabbling schools forget their differences sometimes, and discuss the gloomy future. They tremble for their immortality in the hands of the new generation. There is the hope, however, of being embalmed in an English translation and thus preserved for the ages.

But in the Yiddish newspaper world the problem is much more serious. Authors have nothing more substantial than their immortality to lose. Theatrical enterprises are launched and dissolved each season anew. But metropolitan newspapers are not built for a season. True, their editorial opinions are adjustable, but there is one issue on which they cannot compromise — and that is circulation.

Five Yiddish dailies are published in New York, with a combined cir-culation of over 400,000, representing investments aggregating millions of dollars. Each of them is a great and complicated organization, whose machinery has been evolved through years of experimentation with its particular public. They have branches throughout the country, and the largest of them, the *Forward* (circulation 200,000), publishes special editions in various large cities, maintaining an independent plant and editorial department in Chicago for the manufacture of its Western editions. All of them, however, have sophisticated advertising departments, and the prospect of having their circulation supply cut off, however gradually, can be figured out by them in terms of dollars and cents, the dollars running into seven figures.

So there is a flutter on the Yiddish Newspaper Row on East Broadway, a scanning of specially prepared circulation graphs showing recent and past fluctuations, nervous consultations between the editorial and business departments, the upshot of which is that the editor of the supernumerary English Section for the Young is dragged out of his obscurity and asked to save the paper. Desperately they are seeking succor from the very source where danger threatens.

For though the Jewish birth rate is high, Yiddish is a childless language — bereft of its offspring by the merciless Moloch of the public schools. Every year, as soon as they are of age — and before — in tens of thousands the children are brought by their own parents and offered up on the altar of an alien tongue. Twenty-five years ago it was prophesied that Yiddish would die of this national hemorrhage, but instead the Yiddish press has grown to a state undreamed of then. Where there were a few mushroom sheets that sprang up and died overnight in East Broadway cellars, there are now organizations that can measure themselves impressively against our English dailies. Step into the ten-story *Forward* building, and you will find very little to remind you that you are not on Park Row. Pick up a Sunday edition of the same paper, and its multitudinous folds, including rotogravure, magazine, editorial, dramatic, comic, women's and juvenile sections, are in the best tradition of Sunday-newspaperdom.

Nevertheless, the failure of previous predictions in nowise affects the present situation. An unprecedented flood of immigration that continued until the present restrictions more than compensated Yiddish for the biannual exactions of the public school. But things are quite different now, and would be even if the immigration bars were lifted. For the replenishing flood is drying up at the source. The great nursery of Yiddish, the many-millioned Ghetto of Eastern Europe, has been smashed by the Russian Revolution and the new nationalism which it unwittingly engendered in that area — as effectively as the Ghetto of Central Europe was smashed by the French Revolution and the Napoleonic wars.

A hundred years ago the conquering French army sweeping across Germany opened the gates of the ghettos as liberators. The Jews came out of their thousand-year-old seclusion, rubbing their eyes at the new day; but before they could take in the situation, another tide — the national uprising of 1813 and the awakening of German national consciousness — swept aver Germany and caught them up. That was the end of the German Ghetto. Before that they were Jewish subjects of German princes. Now they had to be Germans.

Similarly, under the Czar, the Jews of Eastern Europe were segregated, oppressed, massacred, but they were not expected to be Russian or feel Russian. The revolution came, and the conglomerate races of Eastern Europe split up into a dozen little states, each jealous of its new-found nationalism and suspicious of all forms of dissent. Suddenly the Jews that had lived for centuries in that territory, regarding it as part of a vague, universal, geographic area called the Exile in which they were merely stopping pending the Messianic era — suddenly these Jews found themselves expected to turn into fervent Poles, Estho-nians, Latvians, Lithuanians, and what not, depending upon which side of the border they happened to be. Many of them objected and became Zionists, deciding that they had waited long enough for the Messiah, and were going to take matters into their own hands. But in large numbers they responded, like their French and German brethren in the past and like their American brethren at present — on the biological principle of protective coloration — by becoming more Polish than the Poles, more Latvian than the Letts, and so on.

Thus, between the Zionists who have no use for anything but Hebrew, scorning Yiddish as the language of the exile, and the assimilationists who champion the particular language of the nation among which they find themselves, Yiddish is left with a dubious future even in its native home. True, in Soviet Russia itself Yiddish is officially recognized by the Government, whereas Hebrew is under a ban. The reason for this partiality is that throughout Eastern

Jewry Yiddish is regarded as the speech of the proletariat, whereas Hebrew has a pronounced nationalistic, religious, and therefore bourgeois, accent. In spite of this official patronage it is foolhardy to think that the new, communistically educated generation of Russian-Jewish youth will cling to Yiddish when Russia and things Russian have captivated the heart of revolutionary youth throughout the world.

The problem is really for an actuary to solve, and it is as follows: If the combined circulation of the Yiddish newspapers is 400,000, and the majority of these readers are over forty, and the only source from which they can expect to renew themselves from the necessarily heavy mortality among such readers is restricted by the 2 per cent immigration law, and if the source itself is drying up — how long will it take for this circulation to be reduced to zero?

But that is not the way the Yiddish journalists look at it. Their solution is the English section, to offset the mortality among their readers by capturing the new generation. That is a problematical answer to a problem. In English the Yiddish newspaper would have to compete with the general newspapers which have shown no objection in the past to catering to Jewish readers. It will actually find itself under a disadvantage in such competition, for the children of the immigrant are not a whit behind in the American disinclination to being different, to having special interests — to being a crank, in other words. Certainly it will take readers with a belligerently nationalist urge to buy such a newspaper, and the circulation of the various English-Jewish weeklies similarly placed is not an encouragement, if it is an example of what an English-Jewish daily may expect.

There is the economic alignment to consider. Three of the five Yiddish dailies are practically trade papers. The bulk of their readers are drawn from the needle trades. These are the Socialist *Forward*, the Communist *Freiheit*, and the capitalist *Morning Journal* — read mainly by workers for its Help Wanted columns and because it is the only morning newspaper. While Jews are still the largest nationality among the needle trades, the balance of power is rapidly shifting. Italians (who are already 40 per cent of the membership), Poles, Lithuanians, and even Americans, are increasing, while the Jews are diminishing. Most of the American-Jewish proletariat belonged to the petty tradesman class in Europe. They became workers by necessity rather than choice, because they had no capital on arriving and were without the necessary knowledge of the new language. They never fancied their descent in the social scale and brought up their sons and daughters to regard " the shop" as a disgrace to which only those without education (graduation from an accredited grammar school) needed to submit. The result is that there are few American-born Jews in the needle trades. Obviously, therefore, an English-Jewish daily cannot expect to thrive on a labor policy. The irony of the future will be that when Yiddish has died out in America the Jews will have become what their grandfathers were in Russia — largely a middle-class group.

Of the other dailies, the orthodox (Republican) *Tageblatt*, the oldest of the Yiddish papers, is practically out of the running; and although it was the first to initiate the English section, there is no future for it in English. The younger generation is anything but conservative in religion and politics. The *Tageblatt* and its coextremist, the Communist *Freiheit*, are lowest in circulation, proving that uncompromising orthodoxy and uncompromising heterodoxy are equally unpopular with " the solid liberal majority " of the race.

The other, the nationalist, liberal *Tag*, would seem — on the face of its editorial policy — about the most plausible survivor in the English future. It is Zionist on the national question, liberal on the religious; and liberal politically, ranking with its fellow Democrat, the New York *World*. Culturally, its comparatively high-brow attitude commends it to the professional and middle-class intelligentsia, bound to be an important element in a specialized circulation such as an English-Jewish daily will have to cater to. It has already inaugurated, as a daily feature on its front page, an English column of Jewish News of the Day. An English-Jewish daily cannot expect to compete with the English dailies for general news. It must expect to be bought as a supplementary paper by those especially interested in Jewish affairs, and therefore this feature of the *Tag* should prove a reliable cornerstone for an English future.

But odds cannot be wagered on the *Tag* without considering the highly convertible texture of the *Forward*, by far the largest and most powerful of the Yiddish dailies Officially Socialist and formerly anti national and even atheistic, it has long been sensing the wind and veering sharply toward nationalism and toward an eclectic liberalism in religion and politics. Its Communist opponent, the *Freiheit*, may accuse it of backsliding; but it is only backsliding with its readers, comprising half of Yiddish-speaking America. Since the Socialist Party is now practically non-existent it may almost be called non-partisan in politics, which gives it an advantage as a national organ over the Democratic *Tag*. Furthermore, an English-Jewish daily, confining itself to topics of Jewish interest and not having to purvey up-to-the-minute general news, can be sold from coast to coast without danger of the news getting stale in transit. In fact, since its appeal will be limited to a specially interested audience, it will be forced to seek out circulation throughout the country. For this the *Forward* is ideally qualified, as it is the only Jewish daily with a really national organization. Putting over an English-Jewish daily will be a difficult job, but with such machineryand resources it may be possible. At any rate the race will be to the strongest, as there will hardly be congregations for all of them in their English vestments.

SOCIAL CHANGE AND SOCIAL PROBLEMS : SOCIAL LAGS IN THE CITY

. . . One can get a better notion of the present plight of the Great City in general if we follow the greatest city, New York, through a series of breakdowns that have attended its growth.

Historically, the first great breakdown of the metropolis came in housing. The crowding of the population into the growing port of New York had, as early as 1835, created a housing shortage and a slum area. Here conditions were so wretched that they drew down the attention of the Health Commissioner; and the Report of Housing Conditions in 1842 was the first of a long list that dealt with the housing problem. It is safe to say that New York has never caught up with its original shortage. Today half the population of Manhattan are living in quarters which are below the standard fixed as safe and sanitary by the tenement house law of 1901: these tenements are within reach of the unskilled worker because they do not possess running water, the heating apparatus and the sanitary facilities which represent the minimum standard for safe living quarters today. But what of the new law houses?'The new tenements meet a minimum standard of sanitation and ventilation ; but they do this at a price beyond the reach of two-thirds of the population; while their bleak courts, their white-washed walls, their dull streets, their occasional glimpse of the sun are still a long way from being the kind of environment in which mothers and children can flourish. Jane Addams showed us a long time ago what happened to " the spirit of youth in the city streets " when it was denied normal outlets for its energy and zest of life; but what have these bleak and overcrowded homes to offer the adolescent boy and girl?

Congestion is such a normal process in the great city, and decent living quarters require such a restriction on the profits of the speculative builder, that even on the edge of the city, where the price of land remains comparatively low, four and five story tenements are erected. Superficial observers talk of this housing breakdown as. if it were a product of the war. On the contrary, there is a chronic deficiency that has been piling up in every great city — in London, Paris, and Berlin, as well as in American cities — for the last hundred years. In the great city there are not enough decent quarters to go round; and even the decent quarters are not good enough. That is the sum and substance of the housing breakdown. In the acutest stages of the housing crises the smaller centers in New York state did not feel the shortage as keenly as the great city. One can almost put the case in a mathematical form: the bigger the city the remoter are its chances of solving the housing problem. This does not, of course, ignore the fact that other causes than congestion have created housing difficulties quite frequently in small cities, and even villages.

The second breakdown of the big city occurred in its water system and its sewers. In 1842 New York was compelled to push back into the Croton watershed for a sufficient supply of clear water, and by the beginning of the present century the shortage threatened so acutely that a new system was planned, with reservoirs in the Catskills and the Adirondacks. If the thirst of the big city is not unquenchable, its tendency to grow has not at any rate been diminished: as a result, the necessity for still further aqueducts has already been recognized. This process must come to an end either when the existing areas have been drained dry, or when the cost per capita for water-mains reaches a point at which water will become a luxury — supplied at an *uneconomic rate* for the same reason that bread and shows and baths were provided in ancient Rome, namely, to keep the population contented. Through this continual reaching back for new water supplies New York City is draining away, quite literally, an essential resource from other communities, dependent upon their immediate supply.

A different sort of loss and disaster results from sewage-congestion. The difficulties New York has experienced in getting rid of its sewage are notorious. The spread of sewage in the Hudson, the East River, and the Harbor has not merely destroyed the opportunities for bathing and caused the practical disappearance of North River shad; it has also, according to the latest report of the Joint Legislative Committee at Albany, cut the city off from 80 per cent of its shellfish, increased the clangers of typhoid (as nearly a thousand cases in the past winter testify) and now threatens the bathing beaches of Coney Island and Brighton.

In this case, the great city can avoid a complete breakdown only by building an elaborate plant and equipment which enables it temporarily to meet the problem. But it does this with blind disregard for expense. The growth of the city might be illimitable if its purse were illimitable, since the ingenuities of engineering can solve many of our difficulties if we can disregard the expense. The point is that the expense is becoming unbearable. The " overhead " of the city is increasing to a point at which it will outmeasure any of its tangible or intangible benefits. Then something must happen: something which will not be more growth and more expense.

We come now to the breakdown of the street system, and the inability of our overground and underground ways to carry the load of traffic. Our older cities were planned for four-story buildings at most. With therise of the six-story building in the middle of the last century, traffic difficulties were felt in the shopping district of lower Broadway. An experimental safety bridge was even built. Today, not only in the lower part of Manhattan, but in vast sections between the Pennsylvania and the Grand Central Railroad stations, up Park Avenue and Broadway, and even over in Brooklyn — *today from two to six cities* have been piled up one above the other. This would be bad enough if only foot traffic and public vehicles were considered: the automobile has added the proverbial last straw, for each car, with its two or three occupants occupies at least twice and sometimes three or four times the space of pedestrians walking. Since our zoning in the built-up parts of the city has all been done in subservience to rising land values, none of our zoning provisions touch this problem; on the contrary, even in parts of the city where the four-story town has lingered, the twenty-story town is permitted — in fact, is being built. If our avenues were wide enough to carry comfortably the present and potential load of traffic, there would not, in a great many parts of the city, be room for the buildings themselves.

Our city officials and engineers are now hinting that the " solution " lies in building overhead streets. But even if it were conceivable that a complete system of aerial streets could be built for the population, this could be done *only at a cost which would fall back upon the land in the shape of taxes — and in turn this would make it necessary to build higher buildings and more streets!* To call this circle vicious scarcely does it justice. In point of fact no large city, however unbalanced its budget, attempts to keep up with its need for free channels of circulation. Every day the congestion increases — in spite of traffic policemen, curb setbacks, one-way streets, electric traffic signals. Even in Los Angeles, whose growth was coincident with the auto, the cars have multiplied faster than the streets have been widened. The and her is already in sight. There must come a time when every street in New York will be regulated as the streets in the financial district now are: individual vehicles will not be permitted to circulate through the business and industrial sections during the day. This is what happened in prosperous commercial Rome when its congestion reached something like New York's present pitch; and it is inevitable here. It is equally inevitable in Pittsburgh's triangle, where it is now actively discussed, and in Chicago's Loop. And all the while the costs are piling up. The hard, practical men who think they can avoid this conclusion while they continue to congest the population and raise the land values are living in dreamland; they simply have not the courage to face the results of their own handiwork.

The breakdown of the mechanical means of transportation follows hard upon the collapse, of the street system; the same causes are at work. As the city increases in height it increases also in area; for the railroad and subway must be introduced to carry the main load of passengers from the central district of sky-scraper offices and lofts to the outlying areas. When the vacant land on the outskirts is filled up, the net result is congestion at both ends. This causes a demand for additional means of transportation. Beyond a point which big cities reach at a very early point in their career, more transportation routes mean more congestion. The only way this could be avoided is by duplicating the existing transportation lines; but this method would reduce the earnings of the existing lines by distributing the load, and it is never even considered except when an equal degree of congestion can be assured to the new line. The cost of all these facilities increases steadily as the lines are lengthened into more remote areas so that in one way or another a subsidy must be introduced to support them at a price per ride the ordinary commuter can afford. At the present time New York, with its five cent fare, is losing more than $12,000,000 annually on the money it paid for constructing subways, and it will lose even more on the new lines, which the transit engineers estimate will be three times as costly.

This is one of the concealed costs of living in a great city; it parallels the hidden cost of other services, including sewers, elaborate street paving and complicated utilities, but all the while this cost is pressing down on the economic well-being of the average citizen. In addition to the half billion or so that New York is preparing to spend in the future on subways, increased suburban facilities are now needed. D. L. Turner, the engineer of the New York Transit Commission, has suggested an expenditure of some three-quarters of a billion dollars, of which he proposes that one-half be paid in taxes, partly by the city and partly by the suburbs; this will, in his opinion, take care only of the increase of traffic in ten years (to April, 1934) when the octopus-city must again face another colossal expenditure, if its bloated growth is to continue. It is possible that the annual saving in man-power, equipment and coal through such a regional redistribution of population as would enable the majority to walk to work, would pay the larger part of the necessary plant and equipment for new communities.

As things go now, on the other hand, there is no way in any of the large centers of avoiding a continuous breakdown in its transit facilities. They are, and they must remain, perpetually inadequate so long as people and industries, instead of being redistributed into planned communities, are sucked blindly into the metropolitan areas.

But perhaps all this congestion is justified by the fact that industry is conducted more efficiently in the big city? Perhaps this more than equals the other losses? Not at all; just the contrary in fact. In most industries it actually costs more to carry on manufacturing on the congested island of Manhattan than it does in smaller industrial centers. The reasons are plain. The transportation of goods through the streetsand on railways is the very life-blood of industry; and in all our big centers these arteries are clogged. Lacking streets to keep pace with the multiple-city, the trueks in New York City spend less time in active hauling than in unproductive work — locked in congested streets, or waiting at the crowded loading stations and stores. The few hours a day that the trucks actually move at snail's pace has already made the automobile uneconomical; and so the greater part of trucking is still done by horsepower in order to lower the overhead charges. The periodic congestion of freight terminals and docks — with the spoiling and rotting of perishable foods — presents another facet of the same difficulty. At the pier, in the railway yard, at the factory, congestion obstructs the normal processes of industry.

Finally, the crowded conditions of the city have increased the overhead within the factory. The garment industry, for example, stands fourth among New York's manufactures; and many of its shops have moved into great skyscrapers in the central district. Here the high rent, the high taxes, and the high cost of fireproof structures have so raised the overhead costs that New York manufacturers, on their own confession, already find it difficult to compete with those in smaller cities, where these costs are lower. The higher cost of housing in the metropolitan area is likewise reflected in proportionately higher wages for the same type of work — or else it is borne by the worker in impoverished living conditions.

Certain industries are inevitably associated with great seaport and traffic junctions, like Philadelphia, New York and Chicago; but as the city increases in population the disadvantages for other kinds of manufacturing tend to counterbalance the advantages of the local market. When the local overhead cannot be shifted, and when smaller centers are, in spite of their poorer financial and business facilities, able to make their industrial advantaged felt, the great city's industries will have to migrate or declare bankruptcy. We are still in the day of postponement; but the day of reckoning will come; and it behooves us to anticipate it. The question then will be whether industries are to migrate into the free area that lies immediately around the great city, or whether it will not pay, once moving must be faced, to locate at some point in a much larger area, where land values are not so high and where a finer environment may be provided more easily, without the risk of being gobbled up eventually — as Pullman was gobbled up by Chicago, and as Yonkers and Mt. Vernon are now being gobbled up by New York in its steady growth.

Inadequate housing facilities, inadequate water supplies, inadequate sewage, inadequate streets and inadequate transportation — these are but the larger and more obvious ills that derive from the congestion of population. They are enough, however, to show that the great city, as a place to live and work in, breaks down miserably; that it is perpetually breaking down; and that it will continue to do so as long as the pressure of population within a limited area remains. I have used New York merely for the sake of concrete example. New York's problem of housing in 1850 was Chicago's problem in 1890; New York's transit solution of 1900 is now Chicago's solution of 1925 — and promises no better; and so on with the other details in the breakdown. Other cities can avoid New York's breakdown only by making an effort to avoid New York's " greatness."

Now all these breakdowns are costly in themselves; unfortunately the effort to put them off becomes even more costly. The result is that money and effort which should go into making the city more livable — the money that should be spent on the education of children, on the maintenance of health, upon art, education, and culture—all this money and effort is devoted to expenditures which do no more than make the physical side of congestion barely tolerable. It is not merely that the effort to supply sufficient transportation routes, to widen streets sufficiently, is inevitably doomed to failure; what is worse is that even if it were successful it would be foolish and extravagant.

If we saw a family with ragged and neglected children,

in a tumbledown shack, half of which was unfit for habitation, spending all its income and savings in providing a tiled bathroom and an automobile, we should conclude that this expenditure was unbalanced: the house should be put in order, the children clothed, the rooms sunned, aired and dusted, and the toilet arrangements adjusted to a decent sanitary minimum. Yet the expenditures of the great city are quite as wild and unbalanced as this. In order to reduce the horrors that result from the breakdown of housing and transportation, the city spends all its funds on futile palliatives. It lives in the midst of a sort of perpetual cataclysm. The great city — if I may sum up the case in a different metaphor — is like a man afflicted with hardening of the arteries, a man so conscious of his condition and so preoccupied with carrying out the incidental medical treatment (hopeless though it be) that he has no time to work, to think, to play, to create or to perform any of those acts which separate a state of invalidism from a state of health.

All the breakdowns we have been studying are the result of a congestion of population; and the greater the magnitude of that congestion the more chronic the breakdown becomes, and the more completely does it embrace all the activities of the city. The big city is bankrupt. The little city that has adopted a program of mere expansion — and where is the little city that does not boast its first skyscraper — is headed in the same direction. . . .

SOCIAL CHANGE AND CITY PROBLEMS : THE SLUM

Man has never built a city of a hundred thousand or more population that did not have slums, those residence quarters from which people flee if they can, where they stay if they lack vision and into which they gravitate if the fates are against them. Every city has its area of poor housing and poverty where society decays like the structures the people inhabit. We Americans talk a great deal and write no little about abolishing our slums. In New York, for instance, there have been hundreds of housing surveys and scores of programs for slum clearance. We have considered seriously every proposed solution from transporting the poor to the country to model housing. Yet we have made no impression on the slums.

Obviously most of this talk is meaningless. The slum is here to stay in spite of the building codes and housing schemes. It is as fundamentally native to the city as the back-yard to the country home. It can no more be wiped out by reform programs than Broadway or the Fashion Center can be legislated out of existence. It is an incident in the building of the city, created by the same general process that gives us Park Avenue and Chinatown. Nor is it too much to label it one of the functional units in the general arrangement of urban life. It is no more the creature of caprice or design than any other area. Neither can it be eliminated by design.

The more we know of all the types of slums the more we realize they are sewed in and interwoven with the larger life of the city. They are segments of that larger life but in no sense isolated. Hobohemia is the most doleful of slums because of its womanless nature. It is an outcast province for hobos, tramps and bums ranging from the never-sweats to the ardent out napless odd-job workers. They are the reserves in the labor market, like gold in the money market. By some strange coincidence the hobo area in most cities is side by side with the banking area. The hobo is the emergency man when short-stake hands are needed for the harvests, the woods, for fishing and building. But he fills emergencies in city life, shoveling snow, working as Santa Claus at Christmas, cleaning yards in the spring. When not needed, he is conveniently tucked away in these characteristic slums for men.

Equally native to the city is the childless couple, in fact urban life rewards the childless couple. Of these there are many varieties from the bon tons on the avenues to the denizens of the back streets, the people who live in suit-cases and feed out of paper sacks. The light-housekeeping slum is the center of chaotic, anonymous, tradition-destroying life. It is restless and transient. Speculation is high, energy is dissipated, the present is paramount. Youth is king in these sections, so convention waits. Frequently there is vice and crime. Low-priced white-collar workers, waitresses and shop girls, the peasants from the American hinterland, the young hopefuls from the freshwater colleges are numerous among the inhabitants. The houses were once the homes of the middle and upper-middle class but now the landlady has converted them into diminutive rooms and takes toll of all who pass. New York's Chelsea on the West Side is such an area and parts of Greenwich Village.

The slums which disturb us are those occupied by the families of small income. Perhaps two million of the inhabitants of metropolitan New York dwell in such areas. Family slums are of many types; those inhabited by natives, those occupied by different national groups and those that are racial, of which Harlem is outstanding. No white slum in the city is more congested or poverty-burdened than some quarters of New York's black belt. For domestic help, for charwomen, for housemen this is the source of supply. What a tragedy to Manhattan if Harlem were moved twenty miles out!

The slum settles where old buildings abound, where rents are low but where space values tend to rise. It is a period in house occupation, the tail-end use of a dwelling. The slum lingers so long as the buildings composing it have residential utility. It has a natural origin, but its passing is less so. It evolves with other parts of the city and is really a consequence of progress. Note Prairie Avenue in Chicago. It skidded in one generation from the matrons to the madams. Once it was exclusive to a fault and jealous of its prestige. Now the city blushes at mention of its name. This precipitous descent of the social scale came when suc-opssive waves of people, each of lesser status than previous occupants, had swept over it. This is the old story and examples can be found in every city.

In the light of experience it would not be difficult to predict the fate of any residence quarter in New York. Take a single family hotel, up-to-date in every respect. In a year it will be twelve months out of date. It will lack some of the later improvements and to that extent be handicapped in competition with the new buildings. In five years it will not only be so much older but five years behind the times. In ten years it will be even less in demand, while in twenty years we should not be surprised to find that the so-called best people had migrated to other parts. Perhaps even the second and third best would not be attracted. That has been substantially the way apartments built twenty years ago have been faring. Where it is quite the proper thing to move with the changing of the seasons or every year, the turnover of apartment dwellers in two decades is enormous. This kind of moving is generally up the social and economic scale. The house is little more than a relaystation used temporarily while the people make their way from lower to higher levels. The house declines in perfect pace with the decline in types of occupants.

This pursuit of status on the part of city dwellers, this press from the East Side to the Bronx and from the Bronx to the suburbs, insures no area of the city against the havoc of change. The object of housing schemes, city planning and zoning is to control and direct the course of change. These are devices for courting the kind of change that is desired and to discourage the embarrassing change. The slum is not wanted but the slum comes anyway because it fits so well into all else that goes to make the city. It appears because it is the dying aspect of city building, as natural as any other form of death. It is an interim between two cycles of life.

A renewal of life is manifest in at least two noteworthy sections of New York. The first is Yorkville on the East Side of Manhattan between Seventy-second and Eighty-sixth Streets where the bottom was all but reached for residence purposes. It had run the usual gauntlet of population successions. Now it is entering a second cycle. One after another the walk-up cold-water flats are being destroyed to make way for expensive one-, two- and three-bath elevator apartment buildings. The remaining part of Yorkville serves as the habitation area of maids, butlers, chauffeurs and other servants for the invading classes of higher status. The second area is the Washington Square section where low-priced tenements are rapidly yielding to select and high-priced apartments. With ordinary wear and tear these will be slum dwellings in another generation. Without great risk one could predict that eventually even the East Side will experience such a normal structural re-birth. More frequently than this renascence for residence the slum is displaced by commercial and industrial occupations. Only in the most accessible places are new dwellings erected.

In any case the use of space is a transient and incidental fact in the cyclic processes of urban growth. It comes and goes with the changing demands for the use of space, and man has very little to do about it. How can he, by taking thought, control such phenomena as rents and land values or alter the natural setting? Yet how they dominate him! Whether he builds a city in Egypt or Rome or the United States, forces over which he has very little control conspire to direct the building. His modern city may be more complex, but all the parts and passions of the ancient city are there. The slum remains one of those incidental parts.

SOCIAL CHANGE AND CITY PROBLEMS : THE SUBURB

The walls of the ancient city enclosed all that really belonged to the urban area. They symbolized a cleavage between two types of human communities, rural and urban. There was no mistaking the limits. Inside was the city, the center and creator of civilization, the trade mart, the refuge for safety, and not infrequently the tyrant of all the region round. Outside was the hinterland that followed and fed the city. Between these inimical segments of society so different in every detail there has maintained an age-old inter-dependency. The country has turned cityward its surplus of goods and its overflow of population; and the city, the consumer of all these, returned its cultural wares and other services to round out and season rural existence.

The country is still rural, the city is still urban and the age-old inter-dependency has not passed, though the city is no longer the compact service unit piling up in tight circles around the market cross. The modern city knows no bounds, facing outward and sprawling in all directions. The lines between country and city have been wiped out by neutral zones that are neither rural nor urban. It is a conglomeration of lesser communities highly specialized and diverse but constituting in their entirety an organized metropolitan unity. Its unity is one of related functions and scattered but equally related parts, of areas that reach at will across the political bounds into the adjacent territory. This is the day of the suburb.

Paralleling the growth of the suburb has gone a re-vamping of urban life. The home has been invaded from so many angles that it has all but lost its traditional identity. The city home has been so stripped and depleted and backed to the wall that in sections like Manhattan it bids fair to lose out entirely. Family life, too, seems to be going by the board. Soaring of land values and pyramiding of rents pinch the city dweller into ever narrowing quarters where for the advantage of location he sacrifices one after another of the comforts of home. The press for space takes away the front yard and then the back yard. takes away pets and plants and penalizes him for having children, soon gives up the nursery. The parlor and sitting room are narrowed and combined. He is forced to exchange the four-poster for an in-a-door bed. The kitchen becomes a kitchenette and the dining room a dinette, while the pantry has all but vanished. The home deoline as family headquarters, as a place for eating, sleeping and passing 1 sure. It becomes a mere address, a place where members of the family leave things they do not care to carry around with them. Unless he submits to the clipping process he must submit to what is more uncompromising, the increasing cost of retaining these ancient comforts. They become luxuries if retained, so ultimately in despair he turns to that residential Eden, the suburb, as an avenue of escape.

The only substitute for escape to the suburb is escape to the street to be caught up in the mechanical treadmill of urban life. Here survival is achieved by gearing in, by getting the pace, by dodging, turning, standing as the noises dictate. In this mechanical discipline the individual is swept along with the traffic through the canyons he built. If he resists he is crushed and if he submits he pays at the cost of his individuality and the theft of his private life. Turning to the suburb is in no sense an escape. He remains urbane as ever, timing and routiniz-ing his life to the pace of the treadmill. He meets his trains with the same clock-like precision he once met the street-cars. It is only the press of in-town homelessness that he escapes.

There are two goals of residential perfection open to the city dweller. He can aspire to an apartment with seven baths on a choice street or he can retire to the suburbs. Either is a cosmopolitan existence but the suburbanite's choice leads to a divided loyalty. He is in the country but not of it. Perish the thought that he should be mistaken for a farmer. Similarly, he is in the city but not of it. In the language of the scientist who classifies specimens, the suburbanite is a border-line case. As a citizen he occupies a unique position. He resides in the country but rules the city. Around New York he lives on Long Island, in New Jersey or Connecticut but his interests center in Manhattan. Out where he lives, and votes for governor, senator or president, he is rarely more than a spectator in local affairs. If he hears that objectionable people are settling near, or that an apartment house is being contemplated on the next block, or that a factory site has been purchased in the neighborhood, he may attend an indignation meeting. He has no vote in town but he belongs to social and civic clubs by which he keeps in touch with things going on. He is a man of affairs in the city and a force to be reckoned with.

For his exodus to the hinterland the suburbanite is rewarded with back yard, with front yard, outbuildings and perhaps a lawn and garden. If he is favored, he has trees and shrubs. In a sense the fence about his lot and the sidewalk in front are his. After a fashion he has neighbors, and sometimes he stops to chin with the man next door about a prize pup, or the weather, or the rotten commutation service. But he is little concerned about his neighbor's business. He never noses about to learn who is who on his block. This, according to his urban mind, is the way to be a good neighbor.

The suburb is more than an escape from discomfort. It is an invitation to exclusiveness. It is this largely at the instance and inspiration of that angel of suburban booms, the real estate man. His efforts in the name of social service and suburban purity are not the crimes they seem on the surface. He is only speeding the inevitable because this is a normal movement. He facilitates the specialized occupancy of residential suburbs. There is a home-owning suburban project for almost every type of city dweller, transporting home-seekers from specific groups in town to specific areas outside. And each of these communities in its own way and for its own kind aspires to exclusiveness.

The suburban migration is nothing short of pioneering. It is breaking with the drifting complacency of paying rent to own a bit of ground. Most of us are over the notion that land hunger is an instinct but we still believe in the sense of security that comes with owning a corner somewhere. Here is something stable to tie to. The individual is less of a mechanized atom in the flux of urban change.

The outward migration of this suburban zone has kept pace with changes in the methods of transportation. The commuter who sneaks of " coming in this morning " once lived an hour out by carriage, then an hour by trolley and now by the aid of the steam road he has doubled or trebled the distance between the office and his home. The rule seems to be that the shorter the commuter's work day and the larger his income the more remote his suburban home from the din of city life.

Residential suburbs are the bedroom towns of the city. There are other types: warehouse centers, factory centers, pleasure centers. The city must be fed, and specialized units spring up at the border. Less than an hour from New York are to be found fishing villages, truck-garden communities, poultry and dairy towns. The city goes to the country for pleasure as well. Broadway is at the point of tensity and congestion but Coney Island is outside and Asbury Park still farther. For the pleasure-loving hotel dwellers there is Atlantic City. Woodstock is an artists' suburb. In New Jersey we find a number of communities to which the intellectual and temperamental flock to be with their kind. The city is sometimes forced to the suburbs for its illicit joy. When a reform wave hit Chicago and harassed the gambling houses and cabarets there was a general exodus to the border, notably to Cicero, which became notorious. Clothing manufacture, requiring little space and much labor, congests near the heart of the city but the textile mills, requiring much space, locate in the suburbs. At the heart of the city we find the hospitals, but sanitaria and health resorts like Saratoga Springs retire to the quiet of the periphery.

The suburb, though it numbers its population in a hundred thousand, is not a city, having no unity of its own, though it may be a significant element in a larger metropolitan unity. There is no point to its aspiring to be a complete community. If it has chain stores but no Macy's, movies but no Broadway, and no metropolitan dailies, it is in no sense a city. If most of its people live part or most of their lives outside, it would be futile to aspire to complete urban autonomy. The suburb no more than the individual can resist the mechanizing discipline of themetropolis. Yet where is the suburb that does not resist the thought of being handmaiden; that does not buck the inevitable to become a going concern in its own name? Witness Bronx or Jersey City or Evanston out of Chicago or Oakland, California.

SOCIAL CHANGE AND DOMESTIC PROBLEMS

No problem in the modern world, perhaps, is fraught with such pathos, such tragedy and such universal interest as the disorganization of family life. And yet in no field of social relations is there a greater dearth of accurate information than exists concerning the steps which might be taken to prevent the heartaches of which each divorce speaks so eloquently. Throughout the western world, and especially in the United States, the sentimental attitude toward marriage has glorified this ceremony until it has become the crowning event of one's life. To break the union, which had its beginning before the marriage actually transpired, represents in many cases the destruction of a romantic picture for which no satisfactory substitute ever is found.

Statistics of divorce and desertion are cold. They offer

little help in understanding the factors which have brought about crises in the marital ventures of so many persons. What good does it do the social reformer or the distracted wife whose husband is unfaithful, to know that in Chicago, for example, there were 6,094 divorces granted in 1919; 2,661 cases heard in the Court of Domestic Relations in 1921; one divorce to five marriages in 1924; and so on? Such statistics give no clue to the causes of the family conflicts which they indicate.

The simplest method, perhaps, of getting at the causes of domestic conflict which tends to terminate in family disintegration, is to study the social life of an area in comparison to that of another or other areas. Thus if the divorce rate is higher in the United States than in Europe, the conventional explanation is in terms of the differences in the cultures of these two geographical areas. But cultural differences in the population do not conform nicely to political or other artificial boundaries, such as state or county lines. Differences in divorce rates by states, for example, indicate the diversity of legal restrictions rather than differences in manners, customs, religion, ideals, standards of living, and so on. If, however, one selects an area within which the terms upon which a divorce may be secured are constant, a state or a city, one may assume that the legal factors represented in cases of family disintegration are the same, and therefore may be neglected so far as a comparison between parts is concerned. Let us take, for example, the city of Chicago.

Chicago, like every large city, is made up of many areas — residential neighborhoods, industrial communities, immigrant colonies, rooming-house districts — all tending to have their distinctive cultural characteristics, diverse by racial and national origin, by economic status, by marital conditions and by cultural type. These cultural differences of city areas are reflected in the activities and interests of the people. Standards of all kinds vary from neighborhood to neighborhood. What is considered moral in an expensive residential district, for example, may be judged immoral in an immigrant colony.

But how do these parts of a city become differentiated? What are the forces making for segregation? What determines the boundaries of communities? How does the process of differentiation affect the family? In what way is family disorganization related, first, to the different ways of living represented by these different communities; and second, to the forces making for the differences between one community and another?

It is said that cities grow like trees, adding new rings at the outer edge and rotting at the core. Yet the growth of a tree is simple compared with that of a city where the processes of expansion are many and complicated.

As the city grows, there is not merely an increase in the number of buildings, an expansion over a larger territory, or a multiplication of avenues of communication. A process of segregation and of differentiation also takes place which gives character to its areas. Institutions and residences spread out in all directions from the center tending always to find the most advantageous position. People arc drawn, likewise, by their interests to the neighborhoods especially favorable for survival and success.

Extension of transportation lines not only draws the outer areas of the city toward the business center in time but it draws business out of the central areas as well. As a result there grows up a series of sub-centers which tend further to break up the community into areas bounded by thoroughfares, railways, street-car lines, bus lines, elevated lines, etc. The city becomes, thus, a net-work of inter-crossing barriers dividing areas each of which has its own peculiar characteristics. These characteristics act as a magnet in drawing those social types of people which are appropriate and repelling those which do not fit. Thus there are family and non-family areas, areas of the rich and the poor, racial areas, occupational areas, and cultural areas. Even the age and sex distribution varies for different areas.

Systems of communication, the newspaper, the telephone, the telegraph, and the radio also have a profound influence upon the growth of a city. They tend to counteract differentiation and segregation upon the basis of external characteristics such as race and substitute for these, or accentuate, the more subtle interests such as aesthetic interests and philosophies of life.

Another factor in the growth of the city is that of industrial expansion. Industries are likely to locate along the rail- and water-ways; light manufacturing just outside the district taken by business; and heavy manufacturing at outlying points. The zone of light manufacturing constantly encroaches upon the area held for residential purposes and thus lowers its value for residence. This causes a selection by this area of those elements in the population who, because of their poverty, cannot find a foothold elsewhere, or who, because of low repute, cannot remain securely in the more favored neighborhoods.

On the other hand, the location of heavy manufacturing at outlying points builds up colonies of workers about the factories, while the managers live outside these districts. Retail stores and other small business ventures tend also to grow up in these sub-centers, producing, in so far as family life is concerned, the same differentiation of areas which characterizes the city as a whole.

Thus in the growth of the city, communities become differentiated— first, in terms of structure which operates as a selective force in the distribution of population; second, in terms of institutions which come to serve the differentiated local groups. The result is to give to the city a wide variety of cultural areas which mould even family life into a diversity of forms.

With reference to family life, five types of areas may be found in Chicago: non-family areas, emancipated family areas, paternal family areas, equalitarian family areas, and maternal family areas. Each of these is closely correlated with a certain kind and amount of family disorganization.

The non family areas are to be found in the center of the city. In and adjoining the central business district — in Chicago, the Loop. They tend to be one-sex areas — predominately male — such as Greektown, Chinatown and Hobohemia.

The areas of the emancipated family are the districts of rooming-houses and kitchenette-apartments, and residential hotels. The so-called " emancipated" family feels itself freed from the conventions which have been the anathema of feminism. There are no children, or very few; relations with the neighborhood are casual, of the "touch-and-go" sort; the interests of both husband and wife lie outside the home; both are employed for the most part, though not necessarily.

Paternal family areas are those of the workers, characteristic of the tenement areas and the immigrant colonies such as the Ghetto and Little Sicily, where the husband rules the home. The families are large. The interests of the wife are confined to the affairs of the home and the care of the children.

The equalitarian family areas are the residential districts wherein live the middle and professional classes. Here there are children, though families tend to be small. There is the maximum of equality in the relationship between husband and wife. The wife has interests outside the home, delegating the care of the children largely to a nurse-maid.

The maternal family areas are those of the commuter, primarily the neighborhoods of the upper bourgeoisie. These cutlying districts are characterized by single houses, typically bungalows, and large yards. There are children here also. The wife tends naturally to become the head of the family, at least so far as neighborhood relations are concerned, for the husband is absent from home most of the twenty-four hours.

In a city the size of Chicago these five different types of areas tend to take an idealized form of concentric circles. The first or innermost circle is that of the non-family areas — the downtown business district. The second circle represents the paternal family areas. In the area land values are high, but the buildings are not adapted to the uses to which the land will eventually be put by the invading commercial and industrial development. Until the invasion is complete, low rents make this district a favorable location for immigrant colonies, rooming-houses and vice. The emancipated family is found here also, though it is hardly characteristic. In fact, the areas of the emancipated family tend to lie along the boundaries of other areas, following the lines of rapid transportation.

How may the varying characteristics of these different family areas help to explain disorganization in the family life within them?

In seventy communities in Chicago, family disintegration shows a range from no cases at all during 1919, the year studied, to 68 broken marriages per 10,000 of population. Here is as exeat, a range in the practice of family disintegration as in the whole of the United States, excluding Nevada. And yet here the legislative and administrative factors are constant while for the United States much of the diversity of rates may be explained in terms of differing legal codes and practices. Those communities with the highest rates of family disintegration tend to form an innermost zone, with a diminution in the rates as one goes out from the center of the city until a band of communities is reached in which family disintegration is infrequent. Obviously, the distribution is not perfect — lines of rapid transportation create mobility in certain outlying communities and increase the rate of family disintegration. Certain immigrant colonies, on the other hand, though centrally located, because of religious taboos against divorce do not show the amount of family disintegration one might expect otherwise.

Chicago communities may further be classified with reference to the prevailing form of family disintegration, as areas of divorce and desertion ; areas of desertion; areas of divorce; and areas of neither divorce nor desertion. These also tend to be found in zones in the order named, proceeding from the center of the city outward.

Comparison of this classification of family disintegration with the earlier one of family areas reveals a correlation between the maternal family areas and the communities in which there is no family disintegration; the paternal family areas and communities with only desertion ; the equalitarian family areas and communities with both divorce and desertion, as well as those areas in which there is divorce only. The emancipated family, being an interstitial group, ecologically, cannot be said to be correlated with any particular group of communities or classes with reference to family disintegration, though divorce is prevalent.

These findings reveal not only the great disparity between the rate of family disintegration in one part of the city and that in another, but also regularity with which family disintegration is associated with certain forces producing mobility, such as: the expansion of industrial organization, the extension of money economy to an increasing number of the interests of life, and the increase in communication and the breakdown of neighborhood contacts, with its accompanying disappearance of the restrictive force of neighborhood opinion. The degree to which these forces diminish as one proceeds outward from the center of the city has never been adequately studied. Yet these differences in the factors of " location " seem to be closely related to the prevalence and type of family disorganization.

In the outlying sections of the city are found conditions very much as one finds them in the country! The family as we know it today developed under rural conditions where contacts were intimate and family status fixed. The center of the city represents the other extreme — casual and formal contacts in which one's dress and " front " determine one's status. The significant thing is that the situation at the center of the city represents only an exaggeration of what one finds in all the areas between the two extremes.

The tendency is for contacts in all areas of the city to become impersonal. The family has not yet adapted itself to this change in social relations and accordingly we see its disorganization on every hand. There are, of course, indications that a new type of family organization is appearing which has adapted itself to the conditions of city life. How prevalent this new form of family relationship has become and how able it will be to withstand the disorganizing forces of city life cannot be said at this time. Statistics of family disintegration show only those cases in which there was a failure to adapt the family relationship to city conditions.

The current cannot be stemmed, as so many reformers seem to think, by going back to old ways and old customs. The only line of progress lies in the direction of an objective study of city life through first-hand investigation without too many presumptions regarding the nature of the problem being studied. The problem of the disorganization of the family is only a part of the disorganization generally prevalent in the city. The family has come to the city from the country and has been disorganized in its journey. It cannot and will not become organized by returning to the country, but only by working out new habits, new points of view, new ideals, adapted to the complicated and shifting conditions of city life.